AuthorHouse™
1663 Liberty Drive
Bloomington, IN 47403
www.authorhouse.com
Phone: 1-800-839-8640

First published by AuthorHouse 4/7/2011

ISBN: 978-1-4567-3485-5 (sc)
ISBN: 978-1-4567-3484-8 (e)

Library of Congress Control Number: 2011901862

Printed in the United States of America

A POETIC JOURNEY
Through a Bipolar Mind

Tina Kaye Hoyer

authorHOUSE®

Dedicated to
My children; my heartbeats
Sarah, Jacob, and Daniel

EVERYDAY

Wind teasing my hair into a frenzy,
At my feet lies a shiny new penny.

Taking me back to childhood dreams,
Yet all I hear are frightened screams.

Childhood memories gone like lightening in the sky,
Yet I have stopped asking why.

No one can know where our journey will lead,
And of whose prey those will feed
And the insignificance of our need.

I rise again from every fall
With head held high and standing tall.

But the twist of fate brings new trials,
And we know not how long the miles.

To be strong for those who love and trust,
Our needs aside for those we must.

For love is stronger than personal gain
And understanding for the afflicted and insane.

To take those we love and lift them high,
And to teach it's wrong to say good-bye.

Love is a strength all its own,
No matter what kind of seeds we've sown.

My life is meant to love and live,
And with all of me to offer and give.

For what else is there in a world of shame
But to blend in without a name?

There will come a day when I will be gone,
And who will be there to sing my song?

All I want for them to say
Is she loved with her all every day.

WHAT I AM

I will never be more than I am;
Whenever I try the door just slams.

People will always judge me.
How do they know? They don't even know me.

Whenever I put my trust on the line,
People are phony and just plain unkind.

It makes me weak and paranoid
When I am around them; it's them I avoid.

I can never fully trust the things in my head;
It makes me sad, and I want to hide in my bed.

Put myself away, away from their stares;
I don't want to be caught in the deception of their snares.

Sometimes the sadness and pressures are the same;
Hiding or exploding for that, what's the name?

No matter what, the hypocrites are the same,
And that to me causes so much shame.

The choices I've made won't go away.
Will I ever be free of the chains in the way?
How much longer do I have to pay?

I try so hard to keep it together.
I have so much stirred up, like a floating feather.

I pull into myself, keep everything in.
There's no one to trust; they fake what's within.

There's a circle around me; don't cross that line.
I won't share with you; what's here is mine.

I can't trust you, the knives in my back.
The bullshit you feed me could fill a sack.

So stay on your side; I'll be on mine.
Looking out sadly, but you won't hear me whine.

Don't make me hurt you; I will if I must.
I'll hurt you with words, for those that I cannot trust.

Trust is hard-earned.
Words will just burn.

I won't let you keep me here in this box;
Just try to corner me and I'll be slick as a fox.

Fuck your words; they mean nothing to me.
I try to fit, but I just want to flee.

You're pushing and pushing to make me fall over.
When will this fucking mess of my life be over?

That was how I thought about myself. I was a scared, paranoid, sad, shame-ridden, broken woman. A year before that, you would never have known that this was the Tina I would become.

The poems I am going to share with you are raw, intense, crude, powerful, passionate, and sensitive. You will be shocked by some, moved by some, intrigued by some, and you will even smile at some. But most of all, you will feel with me; feel what I felt. You will walk with me through my journey from the day I was diagnosed with bipolar disorder until today, as my journey continues. I refer to that devastating day as the day I died; my previous life was laid to rest in the past, and it no longer existed. At times, death would seem to me as a welcome friend.

Most of the poems you will read are from a three-year period during the worst of my struggle with my illness, when I was trying to find the correct course of medication. There are also poems right up to the present day. My life has been, and continues to be, a journey. I learn more and more about the illness of bipolar and myself every day. Although I have endured some tragedies and some difficulties along the way where peace and happiness eluded me, today is a new day; peace and happiness are finally within my reach.

It is important for me to mention that many of these poems have some very harsh language, especially at the beginning. I apologize if they are offensive, but I include them because they are important to express a complete understanding of what I was going through emotionally. You will notice a progression, however; the language will become less harsh, and the poems will become more passionate and peaceful. So please be patient and aware as you walk with me on my journey.

CHAPTER 1
My Journey Begins

In early September 2003, I was diagnosed with bipolar disorder. (Later, I was also diagnosed with generalized anxiety disorder and posttraumatic stress disorder.) I was thirty-five years old, and to me, this seemed like it was the end of my life. In a way, it was the end of my life as I knew it. In the months following my diagnosis, my marriage of sixteen years would end, and my family would be ripped to shreds.

How did all this come about? As I look back now, I guess I can see the pieces to the puzzle being laid out, but the puzzle had no picture. Therefore, putting the pieces together to find the solution would have been nearly impossible. It wasn't until after things began happening that the picture became clear. I had been running this race all my life at warp speed and did not realize it.

By the time I was eighteen, I was graduating high school and beauty school at the same time. I then met my husband, got pregnant, and got married, in that order. By the time I was twenty-three, I had all three of my children, and I was raising a stepdaughter. I continued to work from home, doing hair on the side to keep busy. (As if raising four children wasn't enough.) Eventually, after my children went to school, I went back into a salon, and from there went on to open my own day spa. Needless to say, running a business *and* taking care of a family was quite time-consuming, but

I seemed to have plenty of energy. Sleep seemed to elude me. I was taking handfuls of Benadryl at night to try to sleep; it seemed to be the only thing that somewhat worked. Regardless, I would find myself out in my garden at three o'clock in the morning or on the computer playing solitaire into the wee hours, because it was better than lying in bed doing nothing.

The day I was diagnosed is the day I refer to as "the day I died." It was the end of one half of my life and the beginning of the rest of my life. I became a different person when I had my breakdown, as I call it. It was like a switch was flipped in my brain; I almost had a complete personality change. I became overwhelmingly full of energy, with nothing in particular to focus it on. My mind raced continually with no organized thought, my words were confusing at times, and my logic was very illogical. I began to let my three teenagers run unsupervised. Half the time they didn't even go to school. After having been a very strict mother who kept a very structured life, I began to let their troubled friends move in with us with the idea that I could solve all their problems. I believed I could "fix" everyone. I began exhibiting crazy behavior like jumping off bridges into the river, in my clothes no less. I had terrible road rage; not just anger, such as yelling or cutting someone off. No, I would go so far as stop and get *out* of my car to give them a piece of my mind. I would also go on long drives to no place in particular, and I frequently went hiking in the mountains not caring for my safety, while doing some very risky climbing. I got into chatting on the Internet. This was something that had never interested me before, and it became an obsessive behavior for me. Then I would go on crazy cleaning sprees in my house, out of pure, excruciating agitation. Have you ever had anxiety that actually caused physical pain? Yes, I had it. When you're like that, you must keep moving; that is why people that have bipolar or an anxiety disorder are notorious for going on cleaning sprees or often do redecorating and reorganizing. The only problem is that your brain is so jumbled up that thinking in an organized manor can be difficult; therefore, things usually get more disorganized than organized! I was also moody to the point that no one knew what kind of mood I would be in next, and it could change in a matter of minutes. I myself didn't know what was to come next: a smile, a tear, or an angry rage.

Then the worst happened: I began to have affairs. I had been a faithful wife to my husband, the love of my life, for sixteen years. Now other situations began to present themselves to me, and I believed it was my calling to do them. I even shared with my husband what I was doing. I felt no guilt! There was no remorse or shame; it didn't seem wrong! There were even times I felt like I was *helping* that other person. They were depressed or in a bad marriage, and I could make them feel better. Needless to say, my husband did not agree; this is where things started to go very, very bad.

As things began to fall apart, and I realized I was the cause, I began to get depressed. Yet, I could not stop doing the crazy things I did. I was outrageously flirtatious. Situations seemed to constantly present themselves; I seemed to no longer have a concept of right or wrong. I was like a leaf blowing in the wind, letting each moment take me in whichever direction it willed. I was euphoric at times, never, *ever* considering the consequences. Why? At the time, I didn't even realize there were any. That is what mania is; those are the highs.

Then the unimaginable happened: I began to cut myself with razor blades. When I would get upset and emotional over the things that were happening in my life that I felt out of control of, I did not know how to handle them, so I cut. Cutting on my body seemed to relieve the torment going on inside me. I felt as if there was a huge monster inside (you will hear me refer to the "monster" often in my poems.), and to cut would temporarily let the monster out and give me relief, until the next time. To my great dismay, there were more and more next times. Did I know what I was doing? Yes. So why did I do it? Because my brain told me it was what I should do. There was no need to justify it; there were no second thoughts. I had no conscience thought that I was hurting anyone. I was baffled at the response I was getting; why was everyone so upset? I was fine! I just wanted everyone to leave me alone; I had it all under control. Everyone was looking at me like I had just grown horns, and I couldn't figure out why. When I was on a high, I was having a great time. Then I would come down from the highs and reality would hit. Then the bottom would fall out, and I would be on the floor in my closet with a razorblade in my hand. Those were the lows, and they were unimaginably beyond one's worst nightmare.

MY SANITY

Don't look at me;
I don't want you to see.
Don't look in my eyes;
They may start to cry.

I need to run away,
But I don't know what to say.
You could never understand.
Don't touch or hold my hand.

Stay on your side;
I want to be alone on mine.
Don't you dare cross that line;
Just pretend that I am fine.

The scars won't go away;
I fight them every day.
It makes me tired and weary;
Stay back because you make me very leery.

Don't you see I am all alone?
I won't even answer the phone.
People wonder what is wrong.
If they take the time to listen, they'd hear it in a song.

I write these words constantly.
I keep them hidden close to me.
Would it matter anyway?
They would just walk away and never stay.

My head is all fucked up.
Why won't these meds make it stop?
I can't control it; it's holding me.
Just get away; I have to flee.

My fucking thoughts I want to numb.
Sanity is there; why can't I get some?
This shit inside my head is pushing me over.
When will this all be over?

Maybe it never will.
Just go and take another pill.
My sanity is out of reach.
What happened to what I have tried to teach?

I've come so far, but now it's gone.
Why is everything right now all so wrong?
I have to get a grip on myself,
Or cutting will be my only source of health.

Unfortunately, my cutting became such an effective way for me to cope (even though the relief was short-lived) that it soon became grossly out of control. Not only was it frequent, but the cuts were severe. It began getting so frequent that I was incarcerated in psychiatric hospitals seven times for it. Every cut I made required stitches; there were times I was so afraid of being sent to the psych hospital that I would even sew up my own wounds.

My first visit to the hospital, the visit in which I was diagnosed, was after my husband found me on the floor of my closet, cut and bleeding. That was an eight-day stay. Anger was pretty much my disposition for the entire visit. Of course, I was not the only one devastated by the news; my entire family was in shock. My kids were, along with my parents, my best friend Suzanne, my sister, and definitely my husband. Everyone took it a bit different. My mom bought a book about bipolar and hopped on a plane to Idaho from California to come rescue me. That was the first of many of her rescue trips to come.

My kids, ages eleven, thirteen, and fifteen, who had just adjusted to our move to Idaho less than a year prior, were in shock. They couldn't understand what was happening to their mom. I can't possibly describe to you the feelings as a mother; what it was like having your children walk in to visit you in a psychiatric hospital. What was I to say to them? What does a mom say when her children see her arms cut and stitched closed? What does she do when they walk in and see her sewing up her self-inflicted wounds? What does she do when Daddy is calling Mommy a whore and a slut? What does she say when her children see her being taken away in a police car in handcuffs, not because she did something illegal, but because she is a danger to herself? How does she say good-bye when visiting hours are over and her children want to know when their mother is coming home? What was I to say? We were a happy, perfect, loving family. My children are beautiful, and I love them beyond words. What was I to say when those eyes that depended on me beyond all others were looking at me like all their security in the world had just been ripped away from them? And, it had. Their mom was gone. At that point, the illness was in complete control. I had a long road ahead of me.

HOLE IN THEIR SOUL

Lock the door; hide the key.
What happened to the children that used to be?

Look in their eyes; you can see their soul.
The pain they have suffered has left a hole.

Why is it there? You look at me and ask.
Their mother is gone; she is in the past.

Is there enough time in this life to heal?
It is like we are all in a spinning wheel.

A family there used to be.
Is there a door that hides the answer?
If there is, give me the key.

I am lost in myself, but I see them suffer.
That cuts me deep that my eyes cannot cover.

My heart bleeds for the pain that they feel.
But the pain in me, will it ever heal?

The damage is done; the time it is gone.
It cannot come back; it won't be won.

The hole in their soul, it reflects my own.
All that is come of the seeds I have sown.

I want so bad to take it all back.
The knife it is deep; it's lodged deep in my back.

So what is up around the corner?
Will I forever be a mourner?

What will they say ten years from now,
These children of mine that I've lost somehow?

Will they look at me with hate for the pain inside?
Or will they hold me and love me, putting all aside?

Tomorrow is another day.
Will it be as long and troubling as today?

I cannot say; I don't know the answer.
One thing is sure: the suffering will still be there.

I would take all their pain on my own,
If those seeds from the past could be unsown.

But the past it is unforgiving;
There is nothing that will take away my sinning.

Forgiving me is not the answer.
It won't make this go away any faster.

I guess only time can heal the wounds.
I just wish their pain and mine could go away soon.

The full impact of what I had done had not been realized yet. I was still sunk deep in denial and anger. Bipolar disorder is a mental disorder that can be triggered by many things, and it is also hereditary. We soon discovered that my family on my father's side was infested with mental illness. There were other factors too that we discovered may have contributed to my sudden breakdown. My lifelong battle with anxiety and insomnia had been treated over the last year with Paxil. It is now known that a person with bipolar disorder should not be medicated with an anti-anxiety drug without a mood stabilizer. This proves to be lethal to mood disorders. It was true also that I had been on a crash course for quite some time; I was a ticking bomb.

My anger was crushing. I began to see everyone as an enemy. Paranoia was my new friend. I was assigned to a therapist when I was in the hospital, and she turned out to be my lifeline through this tumultuous journey. When I first met her, though, I must admit I gave her a hard time, but she was tougher than me, and she stood her ground. I figured if she was tough enough to handle me, maybe she was strong enough to help get me through this nightmare I had found myself in. At the time, she became my only ally.

At certain points, I didn't even talk to my parents. I assumed everyone was against me, wanting to take my kids from me; wanting to take everything from me because I was wicked. That's what I felt I was, but I couldn't put my finger on why and what exactly was happening to me. I had so much confusion; my head was in a dense fog. My memory was nearly nonexistent. Lying seemed natural, but I could never keep the lies straight because I would forget what I would say! I could never trust myself; my brain seemed to be an extension of my body that I was completely unfamiliar with. I felt that no one could be trusted. I felt that I had been deceived, and I was being judged harshly. Because I was carrying out all of these horrific behaviors, such as having affairs and cutting on my body, I believed that everyone hated me and thought me a horrible, wicked person. This only fed into my problems by making me more depressed. When I came up from the lows and into the highs everything became surreal again, and I was once again into that twisted way of thinking. I was again having a great time in life engaging in these new experiences. But my highs were becoming less as they continued to tweak my medications, and with fewer highs, there was more self-punishment, anger, and confusion. It was Lori, my therapist/lifeline/friend, who began to try and unravel my mess and put me back together again. Yet, it was in my poetry that I reflected all these conflicting emotions and how I believed I was being judged harshly for my actions. Poems poured from me like a fountain overflowing, as I desperately searched to make sense of it all.

HYPOCRISY

What the fuck are you looking at?
You see the scars my cutting has left?
You look and you ask yourself, what is that?

Don't you judge me in your haste.
You think you're better?
Does your life have no waste?

It's your hypocrisy, you lying your fear.
It's all there; don't you see it?
Can't you hear it whispering in your ear?

I'm so fucking tired of your judging me.
Yes, I have scars.
They show the fear, the tears, and the weakness in me,

Your eyes, they lie when you smile,
Pretending you don't see it.
But your thoughts are adding it up all the while,

Who the hell do you think you are?
Your scars are there,
But yours, you hide and push them afar.

My body, my scars, they are my own.
Each scar tells a story,
Pain you can't understand, you've never known.

I try to hide all that you see,
But hiding is hard.
I wish you knew what it was like to be me.

You spew all your bullshit.
You fake it.
You've missed it; it's hard to hit.

Look at you; look at what I see.
You're a fucking time bomb
But you don't look inside you, only at me.

Damn your thoughts, your arrogance.
What do you have?
Show me what is better on your side of the fence?

My pain may show on my body,
But your attempt at not judging me,
It is very shoddy.

We are all the same, even me; I am no better.
I judge you, too.
It's there, just read this letter.

VOICES

How many voices do I hear each day?
Why can't I make them all go away?

The voice that tells me I am bad,
It brings me down and makes me sad.

The voice that is full of hate and curses;
This voice is just one of my many verses.

The voice of self destruction is strong;
It makes cutting myself not seem wrong.

The voice that says I am ugly inside,
From that voice that I hear, I cannot hide.

The voice that says no one could love me,
That voice is challenged by the need to be free.

A voice that says I can never be strong,
That voice plays in my head over and over like a song.

A voice that taunts and questions me,
Making me feel like I'll never be free.

A voice that says stay away from them;
They cannot be trusted all of them.

The voice that nags and pulls me down,
Making me feel that I am nothing now.

There is also a voice that makes me weep,
Telling me nothing I love can I ever keep.

A voice that says run and hide,
You have no one in which you can confide.

There are good voices too, I must admit.
But where in my head is there a fit?

There is a constant battle every day.
Which voice is here, and which will stay?

Up and down on a merry-go-round,
I cover my ears to block out the sound.

They torture and torment me every day.
I fight to hide them, keep them at bay.

Put on a smile, my happy face.
No one will know, I hide in my place.

Cover them up with a laugh and a grin.
But which voice today will it be that will win?

Going home from the hospital was bittersweet. I was put on a mess of medications, but nothing seemed to be working yet. I was lost in this new world; not knowing who I really was, and not trusting what was going on in my head or even what was coming out of my mouth. The cutting continued. My husband moved into the basement. My boys took turns sleeping with me to try to keep me from cutting myself. My daughter began experimenting with drugs and boys. Psychologically this seemed to be a trigger for me. I was raped as a sixteen-year-old by a boyfriend who decided it was time for me to experience sex. I was young, innocent, and very naïve. I had been raised in a very religious home, and when he forced me to have sex for the first time, I was terrified to tell anyone. I felt dirty and wicked, and I felt like it was my fault. From then on, he continued to force me, using my fear against me and as a tool to manipulate me to do his will. If the fear didn't work, abusing me did. The more I didn't talk, the worse it got. This went on for about a year until I finally fell apart, and my parents found me crying and hysterical in my room. Eventually they got out of me what was happening. I had done some early cutting in those days, but not anything that required medical attention. My parents helped get me out of the relationship, but this boy continued to follow me and stalk me for months after. I would even see him looking in the windows at me in school and following me down the street as I was driving. I was always looking over my shoulder, and I lived in fear and paranoia that he would corner me somewhere and hurt me. So, somehow, as my daughter began to become sexually active, this triggered old trauma in me, which contributed to some of my behaviors and confusion.

I hurt constantly over the pain I was inflicting on my children and family, but my thought process and decision-making skills were so warped by the illness that I couldn't seem to put things back to the way they were before. Everyone was looking to me to make everything right in their world again, and I just couldn't do it! I had always been the strong one, even though my husband Gene and I had always been a united front when it came to raising our children. Now the walls we had built around our castle had fallen, and we were vulnerable to the enemy; the enemy being my brain. There was no longer that unity, and we had no weapons; our world was crashing down around us. In my mind, all I knew was that it was my fault. Through all the therapy and counseling that I have been in over the years, no one has ever been able to convince me otherwise. Yes, I understand that I have an illness, and the things I did were because of symptoms of that illness; yet, the fact still remains that I am the one that did those things, and it was my family that had to endure it because of me. I made the choices whether or not I was sick, and here is where I am because of it. It continues to plague me every day. My poetry still reflects those thoughts, but not as intensely as before because I am trying to let go and just be the person I am now. The repercussions are endless, and I will forever be held accountable. I will accept that; all I can do now is show those around me how much I love

them. Love my children, my family, the man I am in love
with now, and others who cross my path. Yet, forgiveness is
still forthcoming.

MEMORIES

The memories they hurt with sharp pain.
They flood my mind constantly.
But to me it seems like it was all in vain.

How can something so good and so right
Flee away,
And never know there may have been a fight?

If only we could know what is around the bend.
If we did know the answer,
Would it change what could be happier in the end?

Like a child happily eating his ice cream,
Then suddenly he drops it.
The sadness makes him cry out and scream.

There are so many
things I wish I could give back.
I feel like I've taken that ice cream
And thrown it away into a big brown sack.

"You can't have this; it's gone.
You'll never get it again."
The look on their faces,
It will be with me till the end.

That's what I feel I have done to them.
I turn away and cry.
There is no way I can defend.

I want to change what will be.
If I could give back half of what I have taken,
It would make all the difference in the end.

I want to be that mom again.
I want them to depend on me,
No matter where or when.

I want them to see strength when they look at me,
Not weak or sick or fragile;
But strong and safe, is what I want them to see.

I want them to run to me when the world is cruel;
Not think mom will flee to her room
And leave them to stand alone feeling like a fool.

Can I do it?
I know I will try.
There's no turning back.
There'll be no more asking why.

During this time, Sarah was struggling with some adolescent issues, such as experimenting with drugs, and as said before, sex. I didn't at the time know to what extent those experiments went, but as my mother's instincts would pop in and out, I realized the impact that those decisions could have on her future. I look back now and realize that she wanted to communicate with me more than she actually did, as I seemed to be in another world most of the time. She tried to be as strong for me as she was able; we had always been so close, and on the rare occasion that I was in the present, I would help her as much as possible. Here is a poem I wrote for her; I believe she was about sixteen.

JUST AN ILLUSION

Don't you see the seeds that you sow?
Can't you see from them what will grow?

Look at my life; what do you see?
Is that where you want yours to be?

If I could lead you, would you go?
Would you want to hear? Do you want to know?

My heart hurts for what I see.
I look ahead; I know what will be.

Take my hand follow me.
Don't look back, just hold onto me.

How can I get you to listen to what I say?
How can I get you to walk this way?

The corner you'll turn will be regret.
But your course I know; to you it's set.

The life in front of you will be pain,
For upon your head, the hurt will rain.

My heart it bleeds, you'll never know.
I wish I could open it to you and show.

It's like a knife that cuts through me.
Just look my way, maybe you'll see.

The life you live is just an illusion.
All you will get from it is confusion.

Sometimes life will be hateful and cruel.
You're just giving it fire for the fuel.

Please stop and see what's up ahead.
Are you ready to hear what needs to be said?

Your life is so new, problems so few,
But the choices you make are up to you.

You will stumble and you will fall.
How far will that be is your choice, after all.

If I could tell you just one thing,
Take it slow, just clip that wing.

Your whole life, it is before you,
But live them like there are only few.

It wasn't long, and I was back in the hospital. I believe it was
another cutting incident. The medications they had me on
were not helping much. I went through some med changes
that were the first of many, many changes to come. The

second trip was not any better than the first; if anything, it was worse. Let me describe to you what it is like being in a psychiatric hospital; first, here is a poem about it.

THE EYES OF THE LOST

White walls, pink beds,
Nothing here with loose threads.

No dignity, you cannot hide.
I look around, but I am blind.

The cold it reaches to my bones.
We are all here but all alone.

Looking in the eyes of the lost,
And all of us, we pay the cost.

The screams I hear to the bone, they chill me.
Cover my ears; don't look out to see.

The blood has flown down my leg.
It feels like the sadness is a plague.

The numbness wore off; the tears they fell.
Once they started, I could not quell.

My head feels foggy.
My heart feels rocky.

The outside world is far away.
There is no time living this way.

Show me which way I am to go.

My thoughts inside, they are so slow.

My life is gone; it is no more.
Where do I turn? There is no door.

Hide me in this little room,
But return to life, it will be soon.

The loneliness, it aches for the touch it needs,
But that is gone too, pulled out like a weed.

There is a hole in me as deep as a pit.
There is no one to love me; alone I sit.

If my heart stops beating, would it no longer ache?
But my own life I could not take.

.

So back to my room to stare at the walls.
My mind's pictures are there to see as they fall.

The others, they float in a foggy haze,
Wandering the halls as in a maze.

They too have no purpose in this life,
Whether they are brother, sister, husband, or wife.

We watch each other but keep to ourselves,
Hiding our demons we closet and shelve.

The sky outside is gone to me.
White ceiling, bright light is all I see.

I lie on my back; I lie and wonder.
Which face today will I hide under?

Because I was a cutter, I had to be inspected for wounds. I was taken into a small room with a nurse and asked to strip completely nude. I was then inspected to make sure I had no other open wounds on my body other than the cuts I had come in with that were on my arms. She had a diagram on a sheet of paper, where she drew where the cuts were on my body. Whatever belongings I had with me were inspected and taken from me. Shoelaces were removed, as were cords from sweatshirts and any jewelry I might have been wearing. I was handed a toothbrush, comb, and deodorant. They kept my make-up and allowed me to use it if I asked for it, though not without first making sure they popped out all the mirrors or glass.

If someone brought me some clothing and belongings from home, it was also inspected the same way before it was given to me. Shampoo, lotion, soap, etc., was usually kept in the nurses' station with my make-up and used only when I showered. Absolutely no razors were allowed, of course. I think that was the most inconvenient of all; I hated not being able to shave my legs and my armpits! You could forget about blow dryers and curling irons. But, to tell the truth, I really didn't care about those things at that point.

Even personal items like my own pillows or blanket were not allowed. This may seem trivial, but I had a stuffed dog that my son had given me for Christmas when he was nine, and I *never* slept without it; being so vulnerable and helpless in a cold harsh place, I felt the loss of something comforting and familiar in a devastating way. This, of course, did not help my mental state at all.

There were no doorknobs; the only furniture was four beds, one in each corner of each room, a couple chairs, and a freestanding closet with a locker-size portion for each inhabitant's use. In this hospital, you shared a bathroom only with your other three roomies. I have been to other hospitals where the bathroom was down the hall, and you shared with everyone. Since 2003, I have been hospitalized eight times. I guess I've gotten pretty good at adapting to just about any living situation.

There is always a general population room or "day room," as they call it. There is a TV and other things to try to keep you occupied. You are not allowed outdoors except on smoking breaks, and even then it is only for five to ten minutes. The yard is small with very tall gates locking patients in. Meals are served on schedule in the cafeteria. Someone usually yells for everyone to line up and get ready to go, and there is a series of locked doors to go through to get to the cafeteria. Eat what they give you, and do it fast, because you don't have a lot of time. Grab a bag of chips or some cookies to take back with you, because this is the only chance at getting an in-between-meal snack. It's nice if you have someone who will bring snacks and goodies in for you. At least those things are allowed. Most of the times I was in the hospital, I didn't have that luxury.

Then there is time … time moves very, very slowly.

TIME

Time, it moves in many ways;
Sometimes an hour seems like days.
It even creates a cloud, a haze.

Hurt in my heart, the days drag by.
I feel like it causes pain, enough to make me sigh.
I look at others who see me, and I have to lie.
The pain inside, I have to hold back; don't cry.

Time is in control; there's no other way.
How else can I explain? What do I say?
Time creates; it makes the day.

It is out of my hands; it's out of my control.
They say take each day; just let it roll.
They don't understand; time, it digs a hole.

How do I stand? I don't want to fall.
How can I stop it? Who do I call?
I wish I could block it, build myself a wall.

But there is no other way.
I have to wake up each day.
I stay in my bed; I can't just lay.
I have to get up, try to find a way.

When will time be on my side?
Who do I have in which to confide?
The door is closed, not open wide.

Time, its something I will always fight.
Just to me, it doesn't seem right.
But what right do I have? It brings the light.

The light, it moves; it takes me further.
The light, it warms, like a loving mother.

The time, it does what it wants to do.
You are nothing; it doesn't see you.
The giving it gives; it's far and few.

But pain and time, what does it mean?
They go hand in hand, but sight is unseen.
Either one you can control, or so it seems.

So pain holds on, but time will go.
And with the pain, the time will show.
Just hold on, and you too will know
That time is true, and the pain will blow.

On this second hospital stay, my husband was not speaking to me at all. To tell you the truth, I don't even remember how I got any of my clothing and belongings while I was there. My mind is still plagued with huge black holes of memory loss from those earlier days. The day I was released, I called my husband to come pick me up, and he refused. I, who one year earlier was a very successful hairdresser and salon owner with an incredible business, a beautiful family, and a very happy marriage, was now standing in front of a mental hospital broke and desperate with no place to go. I had one friend who I felt at the time I could trust. I called him. He came and got me, but I did not want to go home, so he took me to where he had been staying at the time. The problem was that he lived with some heavy drug users in a house that was known for its drug use. I stayed there for a couple days then I had him take me home. My kids were ecstatic to see me, as I was them. My husband looked at me with contempt, but I did not blame him.

Needless to say, I continued to go to that drug house to visit my new "friends," although I did not partake of the drugs that were offered there. Sometime later, the house was raided and a few of them were taken to jail. The house was closed, and I was very thankful that I was not there that day. There would be many more narrow escapes to come.

At this point, I was so confused by my situation and what I was doing that I dropped into a deep depression. What was happening to my life? Why was I feeling all these crazy things and thinking these crazy thoughts? My mind raced like mad. I was extremely paranoid. I was certain that everyone was out to take my kids from me because I was "crazy." I wasn't even speaking to most of my family or friends. The only reason I was sleeping at night was because of all the drugs the doctors were giving me. I even took to sleeping with my purse under my pillow, because I was paranoid that my husband was trying to steal it from me while I was sleeping. I was also certain that he had my car bugged, and I was being followed. I knew he wanted to take my car away from me so I couldn't go anywhere. Actually, I knew I wouldn't have my car much longer anyway, because we were late on the payments. In fact, we were late on all our bills. Financial ruin was eminent. There was not one aspect of my life at this point that was not in complete shambles.

I would frequently go on long walks. My paranoia plagued me in a way that I constantly thought I heard someone following me or calling my name. I looked around me constantly waiting for someone to jump out of the bushes to grab me. I would go on these walks often and for miles. There was much soul-searching and many tears, and it was on one of these walks that I realized that I had truly hit rock bottom. My home was in foreclosure, my car was being repossessed, my marriage was ending, my children were out of control, I had lost my job, and I was covered in stitches from self-inflicted wounds. What the hell was happening to me? This question beset my every thought.

I started hiding out in my room, where I created a refuge. It became so safe to me that I rarely left it. I was still cutting quite frequently, and I was sewing myself up so I wouldn't have to go to the hospital for stitches. I lived in constant fear of being put back in the psychiatric hospital. I would emerge from my room, which was on the second floor, to go to the main floor to get something to eat from the kitchen, and that was about it. My husband was, at this point, still camping out in the basement. On rare and very uncomfortable occasions, we would cross paths in the kitchen. It was not only strange and stressful, but extremely heartbreaking that this stranger who hated me so passionately was the same man who just recently had loved me so passionately. How did this happen to us? I thought we would grow old together and be happy-ever-after. Yet, when my mania swept me away on that crazy rollercoaster ride, all that pain and emotional turmoil just blew right out the door. All concepts of right and wrong would blur together into a spinning mass, stealing all ability to make moral, rational thoughts or decisions. That was, until the rollercoaster eventually came to an abrupt stop and the mania plummeted to the ground in a chaotic disaster.

During these days of solitude, my children pretty much ran free, although they would frequently come in and hang out with me, especially my daughter. We would have lots of good talks or just lay and watch a movie. My mothering may not have been what it was or should have been, but I was putting forth as much as I was capable of at the time. Even still, loneliness plagued me, lost as I was in my head.

ALONE

Sometimes I look around me and see
Alone is all that I want to be.

Your eyes they pierce through my skin;
I don't want you to see my sin.

I wrap my arms around myself;
Holding me close, I turn in on myself.

Just go away, leave me alone.
My ears are startled by the ring of the phone.

It seems that things are closing in on me.
I turn in and hide; I'm afraid to flee.

Their shouting and screaming all around,
I close my ears to block out the sound.

Don't talk to me; just let me be.
It's too dark for me to see.

All I want to do is hide.
No, in you I won't confide.

Turn away, pretend I'm not here.
Your closeness is only causing me fear.

Don't try to find me, I am gone,
Inside my head, down deep I belong.

No one can know the fear inside.
It's like the sky, open and wide.

My skin is calling to me from within;
Cut deep, it's the only way to get in.

I'm so tired and weak.
Sleep is what I long to seek.

Close off the world again today.
To you there is nothing I have to say.

It is easier to be all alone.
I shake and tremble at the unknown.

I hide in a corner; don't look at me.
Don't come my way; I don't want you to see.

Real life it is just a dream;
Just a fantasy inside, to me it would seem.

CONTROL

My head is full; it's ready to burst.
Which thought takes hold? Which is first?
Sometimes the nervousness makes me curse.

I hold my head; I hold on tight.
What should I say? Which is right?
Why does it seem there's always a fight?

The look on your face is confused; what is it?
Have my words caused abuse?
Walk away, it's okay; you can refuse.

The thoughts in my head are a mess;
Strange and uncertain, I must confess.
I should close my mouth, just talk less.

Have my words caused you to hurt?
The taste in my mouth, it feels like dirt.
Sometimes they're mean, sometimes their curt.

I'm sorry for what I said to you.
My apologies aren't enough; they are too few.
Look from my side; see my view.

I wish I could close these scattered thoughts,
But there is a price; it must be bought.
The battle's not over, though it must be forgot.

Stay away from them, maybe I should.
Then I won't hurt, because I know I could.
This would be better, I know it would.

Why do I have to be this way?
It makes me sad every day.
Hide in my room, so I could just lay.

In my room I am safe and sound.
Somehow, my head, it must be unwound.
Just take my pill; I'll come around.

Controlling my mind with such a tiny thing,
Taking me low, trimming my wing.
Closing my mouth, I can't even sing.
This I must to do to control this thing.

Not only was I depressed, but anxiety had a tight hold on me. My whole life I had fought anxiety. Hypomania is a common symptom of bipolar disorder, and I ran in a hypo-manic state for most of my life. Hypomania is really just a much milder form of the manic state of the bipolar disorder. Let me give you the true definition of bipolar disorder as stated in the DSM-IV-TR (Diagnostic and Statistical Manual of Mental Disorders, Fourth Edition, Text Revision); this is known as the "bible" of mental disorders that psychiatrists diagnose mental illnesses from, according to symptoms. This is what it states:

> Mania, or bipolar disorder (previously known as manic-depressive disorder), is characterized by an elated or euphoric mood, quickened thought and accelerated, loud, or voluble speech, over optimism and heightened enthusiasm and confidence, inflated self-esteem, heightened motor activity, irritability, excitement, and a decreased need for sleep. Depressive mood swings typically occur more often and last longer than manic ones, though there are persons who have episodes only of mania. Individuals with bipolar disorder frequently also show psychotic symptoms such as delusions, hallucinations, paranoia, or grossly bizarre behavior. These symptoms are generally experienced as discrete episodes of depression and then of mania that last for a few weeks or months, with intervening periods of complete normality. The sequence of depression and mania can vary widely from person to person and within a single individual, with either mood abnormality predominating in duration and intensity. Manic individuals may injure themselves, commit illegal acts, or suffer financial

losses because of the poor judgment and risk-taking behavior they display when in the manic state.

This description leaves a lot wide open, as you can see. In some ways it is actually quite vague; but it would take pages to justifiably describe bipolar disorder as it pertains to everyone, as it manifests itself quite differently in each individual. Anxiety, though, is very much a symptom that most people suffering from bipolar complain of; myself included. Sometimes it was almost impossible for me to complete a thought or to keep my train of thought. At times everything was so agitating to me, I felt as if I wanted to scrape my skin right off my body. I couldn't even sit still. As I described, I would go on crazy cleaning sprees through my house, but in such a random order that I almost created more havoc than anything else. I would start cleaning in one area, and before it was even finished, I would start somewhere else. I would have the whole house upside down in no time. For the short time that I worked, if I had time that was not occupied with a client, I was completely beside myself with boredom and feeling like a caged animal. During one of those times is when the following poem was written.

DAMN EVERYONE

Everything looks so fucked up today.
I am so agitated; everything is in my way.
You really don't want to hear what I have to say.
I hope tomorrow will be a better day.

Damn everyone for messing with my will.
You really want to get it; I'll give you your fill.
I wish I could sit and just be still.
My mind, it's racing, spinning like a windmill.

Too much time is on my hands.
Only a few minutes I can hardly stand.
Everyone around me is in such demand.
Will I come down? When will I land?

Don't get in my way; don't cross my path.
All you will get is the lash of my wrath.
Fuck the chains that bind my hands.
I'll take you down; you will not stand.

My mind won't stop.
It spins like a top;
Over and over it flips and it flops.
The words they come, they will not stop.

The sky is blue; the sun it shines.
The peace out there is hard to find.
My mind is in control; it won't unwind,
Just like an old clock that keeps ticking the time.

The drugs I take, they are in control.
Fuck the drugs; I hate them all.
They bind me and slow me, breaking my soul.
They fucking leave a giant hole.

Where is the balance? What is the truth?
Where is the laughter of my youth?

Sometimes my words are hard to find.
They are in a tangle in my mind.
I wish I could push a button to rewind.
Take back some of what was left behind.

Sometimes I feel like I'm in my own hell.
Those days, don't touch me; it won't go well.
Don't even try; I'm in my shell.
I am not buying what you have to sell.

This day will be gone in the morning.
What will tomorrow be? There is no warning.
Maybe the thoughts in my head will stop swarming,
And my heart, instead of cold, will start warming.

I seemed to be in a constant battle with my head; confusion was relentless. Sleep was my only refuge, and I only found solace hidden away in my room. Medications were my only avenue to sleep, so I took them to get there. I was still not finding any relief in the medications other than for sleep. When I was not in my room, I was going out. Not where I should have been going, I must confess. I was doing things I had never done before. I was going to bars. My husband knew about this, of course; I was telling him. I didn't think that there was a problem with this behavior. I can't tell you exactly how I justified myself, but in my mind, I felt that it was okay for me to be married and to go out to bars and meet men. I told him everything that I was doing in the beginning. Once things got out of hand, and I realized it caused problems when I told him, I stopped telling him. I began to lie. Once I started lying, I lied about everything. The only problem with this was that I could never remember what I said. He knew what I said, so it was absolutely ridiculous that I even tried to get away with anything at that point; but this never occurred to me at the time. I was lost in some crazy little world of make-believe, and I was spinning this lopsided web that would never hold up. Sometimes I would wonder why my husband would look at me with this wild look on his face like he didn't even know me. Now I know why; he didn't, and neither did I, for that matter.

I wrote constantly. In my journals, I would write random words describing my feelings. If I was angry, they would be giant scribbles of foul language across the pages. If I was depressed, they might be scribbles of sad words or phrases of depressing thoughts. There are also several unusual poems of short sentences, like the following, which is simply called, "Words."

WORDS

SLEEPY EYES
MY HEART CRIES INSIDE
SADNESS CRAWLES OUT
I WISH I COULD SHOUT
MY MIND PLAYS TRICKS
IT'S FOOLING ME OUT THERE
DO YO LOVE ME?
CAN YOU POSSILBLY?
I AM REACHING OUT
BUT I TAKE IT BACK
I WANT TO BE ALONE
INSIDE OF MYSELF
DEEPER I CAN GO
MORE THAN YOU'LL EVER KNOW
MY SKIN CRIES OUT
IT'S TOUCHING ME
MY HEART SAYS NO
BUT MY MIND IT SAYS YES
WHAT DO I BELIEVE?

WHICH WAY IS BEST?
WORDS MEAN NOTHING
THEY CAN'T DESCRIBE
MY HANDS ARE TREMBLING
LIKE THE PAIN INSIDE
MY BODY IT ACHES
THE FIGHT MAKES ME WEAK
SLEEP … I WANT TO SLEEP
GO AWAY
DON'T TRY TO GET IN
TOUCH ME, AND I WILL WEEP
FEEL MY HEART BEAT
IS IT STIL THERE?
DON'T REACH OUT TO ME
I NEED TO BE FREE
DON'T TOUCH MY SKIN
IT'S ON FIRE
IT BLEEDS
YOU'RE SO FAR AWAY
DO I WANT YOU TO STAY?
SOMETIMES I FEEL YOU
LIKE IN A DREAM
THE RIVER IT TAKES IT AWAY
TIL IT'S A TRICKLING STREAM
I'M LONELY
DO I WANT TO BE?
ESCAPE IS THERE
WHEN THE DOOR IS OPEN
WHO HAS THE KEY?
MY FEAR IS COLD
CLIMB OUT OF THIS PIT
MY BODY FEELS SO OLD
SLEEP AGAIN
TAKE ME AWAY

CAN YOU SAVE ME?
DO YOU WANT TO STAY?
WHAT IS HOLDING ME HERE?
I CAN'T BREAK FREE
GET UP
FIND A PILL
SWALLOW
SLEEP AGAIN.

Anxiety continued to be an enormous problem for me; it is still, even now, my most difficult symptom to handle. My anxiety can get so bad that it will cause an anxiety attack which will, in turn, occasionally cause me to faint. During that time of my life, though, I would get so tense with anxiety that I would just pace and pace, if I was indoors, like a trapped animal. To deal with it, I would go outside and just walk. It didn't even matter what the weather was like. Snow or rain was fine; if it was hot, I would try to walk near the river if I could.

By now my husband and I had separated, and he had moved out of the house; the kids were living in the house with me. It was the beginning of winter, and it was cold. Gene, my husband, was living out of the back of his truck. He had turned into a very angry person at this point. I'm not saying he was wrong or right in the things he did to me at this point, but I do understand. He was hurting beyond measure, and punishing me was the only way for him to relieve some of the anguish he was experiencing. And punish me he did. He closed out our joint bank account so I no longer had any access to money. I was pawning CDs, DVDs; everything I could just to buy groceries and gas. He stopped paying the utility bills on the house. The temperature in the house was forty-nine degrees at times until I got help to make the electric payments.

One morning I was awakened to screams from my daughter. I ran down the stairs to find Gene coming out of the bathroom where he and Sarah had been fighting. He had hit her, and upon my arrival, she quickly ran to her room and called 911 as Gene turned his rage on me. He came at me, and I stepped back preparing to be hit also. Instead, he slammed me against the wall, hard enough to cause injury to my neck. Unfortunately for him, we literally lived right around the corner from the police department. They had already arrived. Although Sarah and I were shaken, we were not going to press charges, but Gene had already admitted what he had done, so they arrested him. The next day I filed a restraining order. This was not the man that I had loved. What had I done to him?

On the days that I was reality conscious, I knew that I was at fault for pushing him to this point. On bad days, I was enraged at him for what he was doing. Needless to say, two weeks later, I dropped the restraining order. In the order, I only wanted him to stay away from the house, but it also included the children, and I did not want to keep him from them. Disregarding what had happened between him and Sarah, he was, and still is, a great dad.

I thought things were crazy enough in my life, but I made things even more complicated by adding another man. As I said, I was beginning to hang out occasionally at bars. We were living in a very small town in Idaho, and there was a local bar I would go to once in awhile. One night I met a man; his name was Lee. He was quite intimidating to look at with his shaved head and tattoos, but he was singing and playing the guitar in a way that softened his demeanor. Coincidentally, I was sitting with a friend of mine who was sitting with another friend, who was friends with Lee. When he was done singing, he came over to our table and introduced himself to me. We sat at that table and talked until closing. That conversation sparked a relationship that haunts me to this day.

TOMORROW IS KNOCKING

Time, it turns in a circle.
We see the backside as if it's a miracle.

Where does time go tomorrow?
What happens to today's sorrows?
Can we have some just to borrow?

The lines on our face tell the day.
What is there to do? What to say?
If only we could stop it make it stay.

Close the door; don't let it in.
Don't let it tell of our sin.
I don't want to know where I have been.

Tomorrow is knocking on the door.
I hold on tightly to my deepest core.
I don't want tomorrow to come anymore.

It's ruthless; it's unkind.
It steals from your mind.
Please hold it; just keep it behind.

Tomorrow brings new sadness and pain.
It brings agony for the insane.

For those, what is there to gain?

Let today last forever; don't take it away.
This is my plea; it's what I have to say.
Tomorrow won't be just another day.

Our relationship lasted eight months. He moved in, he moved out, and then back in again. For the most part we were very happy, until the last couple of months. Then things started to make an unusual change. Lee was one of four brothers from a very disturbed household. His mother was a very depressed woman, who found child rearing extremely exhausting and had a hard time coping. His dad was away often with his work, but when he was there, he was extremely strict and hard on the boys, to the point of being abusive. Lee himself was a very disturbed individual. He was an ex-con who had done twenty years in prison for numerous counts of armed bank robbery. Of course, at the time, I was not too mentally healthy myself! In fact, everyone that knew me could not understand what I was doing with a man like Lee. My attraction to him was certainly not a normal one; aside from the fact that I was married, circumstances in my life were anything but normal.

In defense of Lee, though he was a very disturbed man, he also was a very loving, sensitive, caring person. He loved to laugh; he was funny, and he enjoyed life. He was an amazing artist. His drawings are incredible. He was also a tattoo artist; at one time had his own tattoo shop in town. He was a beautiful songwriter and singer; he even wrote two songs for me.

Lee had some habits that I was unaware of. Toward the

end of our relationship, as things began to unravel, it started to show. We lived together for about six months off and on, and I believe these habits were the reasons he moved out each time. Lee was using methamphetamines, and he was very secretive about his pornography use. He also liked to go out drinking late at night. I think he liked living alone so he could come and go as he pleased and not have to answer for any of these behaviors.

One day I got a very strange phone call. It was the police, and they said they had pulled Lee over for driving while intoxicated, and he had my dog in the back of his truck. Odd, since my dog was in the backyard. So I drove down to where they had Lee pulled over. (Being a small town, it was right around the corner from my house.) Lee was completely out of it. I just assumed he was drunk, which was unusual for him in the middle of the day. From what I had seen, Lee hadn't shown me that he was a big drinker.

Nope, it was definitely not my dog; it didn't even look like my dog! So they took Lee to jail and the dog to the pound. I went and bailed Lee out of jail, but by the time I actually got him, it had been hours. I thought that he would have been somewhat sobered up by then, but he was a mess! I determined very fast that he was not drunk; he was either on drugs or something mentally had seriously gone wrong. He did not even know me. He stood talking to the police officer who brought him out to me for a good three minutes before he even saw me, and when he did, he introduced himself to me. I was horrified! I managed to get him into my car, but it was tedious at best. He was in another world. I decided I was taking him to the hospital, but I made the mistake of telling him so. He freaked out on me and became belligerent. I managed to calm him and get him into the seatbelt. He kept going back and forth between drowsy and belligerent. When he was belligerent, he would try to get

41

out of the seatbelt and say he was going to jump out of the car. I had to drive with my hand over the seatbelt hook so he couldn't unhook himself.

I finally got him there and left him in the car to go tell the nurses what they were going to be dealing with. They called the police when they heard that he had just been released from jail. We did nothing until the police got there, but once they did, I told them to just let me walk him in so he wouldn't freak out when he realized that they were there. They agreed, and as I suspected, he did fine until he saw them. When he did, he just went ballistic. He ran. They chased. He ran. They tased. I screamed. It was horrible. They had him on his stomach and hog-tied in no time. The psychiatric hospital would be his next stop. From that day on, Lee never recovered. Suicide was all he would talk about.

He became extremely moody, anxious, and depressed; all the things that make up a very unstable person. He spent some time in the psychiatric hospital. I brought him Burger King, his favorite, to try to cheer him. He cried a lot. After that, though, he seemed to get more heavily into his drugs. (I can see now as I look back.) He began picking fights with me for no reason, and he stayed mad, whereas before, he would get over things very easily.

Sometimes I seem to have a sixth sense about things. At some points in my life, it has been sharper than others. At that time, it seemed to be particularly sharp. I wrote the following poem called "Suicide." When I read it to him, he cried and cried. Sometimes I feel like maybe I pushed him over the edge. All I wanted to do was to make him see what it would feel like to be the one left behind.

SUICIDE

I look in your face; you don't see me anymore.
What were you doing trying to even the score?
The fight in you must have felt like a war.
The blood runs slow, there is life no more.

Why didn't you tell me? Couldn't you say?
Which direction you needed, where was the way?
If only I could have just had one more day,
I could have saved you; I promise I could make you stay.

The anger inside me, it burns like a fire.
You fucking left me here, hanging on a wire.
Don't you know that I, too, sometimes tire?
But you promised; now you are a liar.

If I could say one more thing to you:
Don't shorten our days; they're already too few.
Your life could be more; it could be something new.
What am I left with? What can I do without you?

You're selfish and angry, but what right do you have
To take from me the life and love that we had?

My heart is in pieces; it's on the ground.
I look at them and say, there's nothing to be found.
I can't put them back; I can't go another round.
I have no strength; it can't be rewound.

I hate you for this, but you can't come back.
Fuck you! Look at me, I'm dressed in black.
What was it I couldn't give? What did I lack?

I will never forgive you for leaving me behind.
If only there was a button to push and rewind,
I'd hold you and love you, give you peace to find.
I'd break you open, look deep into your mind.

I'd find the part that took you away.
I'd stomp it and kill it, making you stay.
See how you feel; see what you'd say.
I would not let go; I'd push everyone away.

But it's too late now; that time is gone.
Couldn't you wait? Just sing me another song?
What was in you? What was wrong?
The time before me now, it's much too long.

I can't be without you, this is true.
The blood in my veins, now it flows, too
In a few minutes, I'll be with you.
I'm sorry for the ones I left behind, just like you.

I had been working in another salon for a few months. It had
been going pretty well. Lee had been working at Wal-Mart in
Boise. Then, one day he just walked out of his job. He didn't
tell anyone why or that he was even leaving; he just left and
never went back. One day we were driving, and he picked
another fight with me. I was completely dumbfounded. I
didn't even know what to say to defend myself; he just got
more and more angry. I thought he would get over it. We
went to bed, and I went to work the next day.

I came home from work, and he was watering the roses.
I thought he was probably over it by now. As I approached

him, he turned to look at me; he face was menacing. His countenance was nothing like I had ever seen before. He definitely was not over it. I was chilled by his demeanor. I merely said hello to him and went into the house. I had remembered a time about a month before when we were coming home from vacation. Lee had threatened to kill Jake and I while we were driving down the freeway. He had gotten angry at me, and said he was going to kill all of us by driving the car into oncoming traffic. Now I had a feeling of foreboding that chilled me to my very core. At that moment, I packed a bag and waited until I could get away. Shortly thereafter, Lee left to go to the store for cigarettes. I got into my car and got out of there as fast as I could. I called my kids and told them not to go back to the house, and I headed for Oregon to the same friend who picked me up from the hospital on that very lonely day. James was his name, and he had bailed me out of trouble more than once in those days.

When Lee found out that I had left, the news did not go over very well. He called me and told me that when he found me he was going to kill me and then kill himself; and he *would* find me. I had many phone calls that I kept recorded on my phone, threats he made to my life. I believed every one of them. I knew if he found me, he would kill me. The day after I left, so did he. I was gone for five days, and then I decided I had to go home. I had left my job, and I needed to get back.

Lee had gone to Las Vegas; I tracked him by following his use of our bank account debit card. One day the debit card quite suddenly stopped being used; no more gas, food, nothing. I thought that maybe he had actually killed himself. I was a terrible mess! I was afraid for my life, I was afraid to go home, and I couldn't help but be worried about Lee. I was still battling medications and the symptoms of my own illness. My emotions were on a spinning rollercoaster. Then I found out that my dog had been taken to the pound because he was disturbing the peace. (My neighbors hated us. We were Californians, and we had teenagers. Not a good combination for a small conservative town in Idaho.) They called the cops on my dog. Believe it or not, this is what finally pushed me over the edge. I went on a cutting spree and ended up in the hospital again.

Lee reappeared. He came home and found out where I was. Somehow this is what finally pushed *him* over the edge. He went out into the hills, sat in his truck with a hose running from his tailpipe into the cab of his truck, and slowly died from carbon monoxide poisoning. Some people on horseback found him; it looked like he was sleeping peacefully, but he was gone.

I still had to be told. I was taken into a small room and given a small cup with two round white pills. Funny the things you remember; I will never forget what those two little pills looked like in that tiny cup. I knew as soon as they gave them to me, but I took them anyway. Then they told me. I was put on suicide watch for the next twenty-four hours.

Poems poured out of me. You tend to put aside a lot of the bad things about a person after they are gone. You remember more of the good things. I have seen that in people who have lost loved ones. I particularly saw that in my grandmother when she lost my grandfather ten years ago. Yes, in the end Lee did want to kill me, but that wasn't the Lee I loved; the one I loved was tender and sweet and was in love with me. He didn't want to hurt me. That Lee was a sick Lee. Now he is gone. My poems about him reflect every single emotion of my grieving stages, from anger to sadness and everything in between. For a while it seemed I couldn't stop expressing my grief in my poetry. While I was still cutting, I believe that if it were not for my writing, I would have probably been doing much more cutting than I did.

MY RAGE

My body aches for your touch.
My soul aches for its mate so much.
I feel like I have lost my crutch.

Please come back to me.
I'd do anything, you'd see.
What can I do to make it be?

My heart has been ripped from my chest.
I try to live each day to my best,
But they are sadder and sadder than the rest.

Everything around me reminds me of you.
The love I had for you was so strong and true.
Now my days are long and blue.

Why was your hurt so deep and dark?
Or was it some way for you to leave your mark?
You stripped me of our love, leaving me so stark.

I clench my fists and rage at you.
Were you angry and raging at me too?
What were you thinking, or were your thoughts few?

Did you really love me like you said?
Did you really mean the love we shared in bed?
Was it all a bunch of bullshit you fed?

I believe that you truly loved me.
But maybe your love was lacking, and you didn't want me
to see?
It doesn't matter how you loved me, I just wanted it to be.

Now I am alone and empty.
Everything is you, don't you see?
We shared every part of our life; now how will it be?

Please come back; fill my soul,
All that is left of an empty hole.
The pain inside is unbearable.

I will love you till the day we meet again.
I just wish I knew how and when.
Please come to me; let me know how it will end.

I am left here to go through this life;
The life that was supposed to be as your wife.
Now my pain, it's a dagger, a knife.

Stay close; don't go away.
Be at my bed as I lay.
My heart I give to you as I pray.

IN YOUR EYES

I found a picture today.
I looked in your eyes. What did they say?
I saw your soul, a tortured man.
Why couldn't you make it when you said you can?

Deep and dark is what I see.
No one knew what your life could be.

You were hiding from your ghosts.
No one knew the pain inside you; you were just a host.

Things in your head you stuffed away.
If you fixed them, could you have stayed?

Were there too many horrific memories you could not
hide,
To the point that even to me you lied?

Are you free now?
I wish I knew how.

I miss your laughter and our love.
I know you're there floating above.

KISS ME GOOD NIGHT

I cannot feel; I am numb inside.
This place I'm at, I can no longer abide.

If you reached in and touched my soul,
It would not be there, only a hole.

The soul I had was taken by its mate.
Who could understand the test of this fate?

Two souls searching in the blind of the night,
Will they meet again? Maybe they might.

Until it is returned to me, my soul is lost.
The test that has been put on us has left a heavy cost.

All that is there is numbness now.
I cannot feel it; I don't know how.

Others through life will try to fill.
Most will fail; I know they will.

There is only one with the perfect fit.
The rest, they try to stuff you only with bullshit.

For that, I will not allow.
Maybe the one, he will return, but how?

I will wait, and I'll wait; where is the end?
Who to my heart will my soul send?

Fly in the night; kiss me good night.
Don't forget me as you pass in flight.

Remember I loved you more than any other.
But you left me here alone, my tears to smother.

I wipe them dry time after time, every day.
People look at me; they don't know what to say.

Touch my lips, as you pass, my love.
For that you will be, forever, my love.

YOU ARE GONE

You are gone. Why did you leave?
I thought that to me you would always cleave.
Our life together, I thought we did weave.

The demons inside you, you could not break free.
I am sorry, to my eyes, I did not see.
And now this is where it has led us to be.

Where from here do I have to go?
What happens now to the seeds we did sow?
I look around me and everything dies slow.

The life we planned is but a memory now.
It was taken from us; I don't know how.
But what life gives us, we can only allow.

I will miss your face that smiled for me alone.
I will miss the part of you that to only me you did show.
I will miss your soul that the wind has now blown.

Never will I feel the touch of your skin.
Never will I see your fight and strength to win.
Never will I believe that what you did was a sin.

I hurt inside for the pain in you
That led you to this thing that stayed in your view.
Our time together, it was much, much too few.

Eight months of your life you did give me;
Every single memory will always be with me.
Every look in your eyes will I forever see.

I wish I could hear one more time that you love me.
I wish one more time, my love for you, you could see.
Now memories of that love shared is all we will be.

I know that you know no one loved you like I.
I hope you carry it with you as your spirit will fly.
But I cannot help the pain I feel as I sit and I cry.

I will miss you beyond measure, this is true.
For there was no one on this earth that was like you.
Just know wherever you're at, that I will always love you.

SOME DAYS

Some days are slow, and your face fades.
Then some days your memories in my heart they wade.
Some days remind me of the life we laid.

Can't the days go by faster to free me?
I can't stand that I am an I and not a we.
Your face and touch and smell will never again be.

Some days I cry and miss you more than life.
Some days I hate you and curse that I would have been
your wife.

I hate you and fuck your name with everything I am.
But some days I'm soft and vulnerable as a lamb.
Then I look at your picture and miss you; it hurts like a
slam.

I will never know the answer to my questions today.
Everyone looks at me and doesn't know what to say.
There will be a day that I will see you again, I pray.

What am I supposed to do? Where do I go?
With my life now, I think about and do not know.
It seems like this point of my life is so low.
With you, I know together old we will never grow.

My heart seems that it will never heal.
My head spins like a fast rolling wheel.
What happened? What about our deal?

You broke it; it's gone now.
Damn you! Fuck you! What do I do now?
Do you see me? What do I do? Tell me how.

I try to push you away,
But then I break and want your memory to stay.
Every day is new; I see it in a different way.

Other men, they come and they go.
They are not you; this it does show.
Will I love again? Do you know?

None of them are ever like you;
Some come close, but only a few.
I don't want them; I don't want something new.

Your love was intense; it was strong.
Each one falls short; something is wrong.

My gut, it rolls inside.
The pain is deep, and it is wide.
Sometimes I think I want to be on your side.

What is stopping me? Do I dare?
Only my kids, they would care.

But I know my family, they would fare.
Selfish, I know, but it does not matter.

Sadly, my children were so negatively affected by this relationship that I can't blame them if they never forgive me for putting them through that whole horrible ordeal. My daughter, Sarah, and I recently had a conversation about it; she is still very disturbed by the presence of Lee in our lives. He did not treat them very well, although he never abused them. I believe that Lee was not meant long for this world, and due to his extensive stay in prison, he had become institutionalized and did not truly understand how to cope in the outside world.

The night that Lee came home and found me still gone, Sarah was the one that told him that I was in the hospital and expressed her anger toward him that he was the reason that I was there. She was very brave to confront him as she did, but that is my Sarah.

Jake was also very affected by Lee. First of all, he was the one in the car when Lee threatened to drive into oncoming traffic and kill us all. Jake had a fear that Lee would hurt me; he was very protective of me already. He was that way even as a young boy; always his mother's keeper. I feel an extra burden of regret in regards to Jake and that day I left; I left Jake at the house. I did not fear that Lee would hurt him; Lee would never have hurt any of the kids. He actually cared about them a great deal. I was his focus, but to Jake it must have felt like abandonment. In my messed up mind, just telling the kids to stay away from the house seemed to be sufficient. Now I can't even imagine that I could have left them to their own defenses.

I have so much self-loathing for ways that I handled some situations. I spun some very tangled webs, and when you're in the middle of that web, it's hard to see a clear path out. The decision-making part of my brain was one constant misfire. Reality was completely out of my reach at times, and it was usually the most crucial times. I felt my children were lost to me and that they would never forgive me for the trauma I put them through. Their perfect, secure lives had been shattered like a beautiful glass window. I doubt they will every fully recover. And for this, I doubt I will ever be able to fully forgive myself.

I'VE LOST THEM

Why do they hurt me? Why must it be?
Isn't my pain enough for them to see?
I know that our family is no longer a we,
But why is it me they hurt? Can't they see?

The mother I was is gone in the past.
She went far away all too fast.
How long will the hurt be? How long will it last?
I can't help what's happened to me in my past.

They blame and they accuse me.
The anger, it's towards me.
Sometimes I want to run away, just turn and flee.
When will it stop the hurt directed at me?

I try and I try to make things right.
Every day is a battle; this is always a fight,
Even when I try with all my might.

What is the answer? What should I do?
Can't tomorrow be better? Something new?

My children, I've lost them, by my own sin?
How long will they punish me? Can I ever win?
Where is the strong me? Where has she been?

I can't be strong; my strength is gone.
My weakness they see, and it's me they prey on.
What will be next when I face the new dawn?

Close my eyes; fist my hands.
I feel I've been tied up in heavy bands.
The ride I'm on, will it never land?

My insides, they're balled up and tight.
My will is gone; I don't want to fight.
Not anymore can I use my might.

Take it away; close me off from the world.
My fist, my hands, can't be uncurled.

Someone else step into my place.
I am giving up; just look at my face.
The tears that flow, they are a waste.

My want to be, what I need to be,
It's all gone; I can no longer see.
Just let me go; give me a place to flee.

A short time after I was released from the hospital, I went to the police station to talk to the officer who spoke with the very distraught Lee, on the afternoon preceding his death. I was not pleased by what I heard. I also was very angry at his parents. They had already shown how insignificant their children were by the way they treated them in the past. Now that Lee was gone, the way they marked his passing was a further sign of how little they cared. When I was released from the hospital, three days after his death, he was already cremated. His obituary was a mere three lines that told nothing about what he left behind, and there was not even a memorial service to commemorate his life. I am quite certain that his remains are sitting in a jar in the corner of his mother's kitchen next to his dead brother, the other brother that committed suicide from depression. He was gay and was extremely ostracized by his family, particularly his father.

From these two injustices that I felt came these quite harsh poems, or letters, if you will. They are probably the angriest poems I have ever written, but don't worry, even though they are letters, I never sent either one of them. This was merely a therapy or a coping skill for me, part of my grieving process. The first poem is to the officer who talked with Lee the night Lee took his life. This officer walked away knowing what Lee's intensions were, and he did nothing to try and help or to stop it. I could not then and I do not now understand how any human could walk away from another human suffering in such a way. From what I understand about law enforcement, mostly based on my own experience, if someone is threatening to harm themselves, they must be taken in for a psychological evaluation. They are never just left alone after threatening to harm themselves or someone else.

The second one is to his parents; it is very self-explanatory. Once again, I will warn you: these are very explicit. Grief is powerful, and the anger that goes with grief is very consuming, but writing was a good outlet for me, and it helped immensely.

A LESSON FOR YOU

So what is it exactly in that oath you take?
I thought it was to honor and uphold justice to make.

So how do you feel when you have failed?
When the one who loved him has sat and wailed?

Because of a choice that you have made;
Because to you someone's path had been laid.

So fuck you for thinking you're God.
You're just a teenager spewing his wad.

But you, you have to sleep at night;
So in your head is there a battle, a fight?

Do you awake and hear my screams?
Do you see his dead body in your dreams?

He was nothing to you, or so you thought.
All the lies and bullshit, you bought.

You could have helped; you could have stopped it.
But to you, an ex-con, he was worth shit.

Where will you be on judgment day?

Open your mouth; what will you say?

A life saved that day, you could have said.
But you toss and turn and squirm in your bed.

Will you look at him and say, "I didn't know"?
Fuck you, for his life you did just blow.

You'll get yours; it'll come back around.
I hope I'm there; I'll hear the sound.

Will someone be wailing for you in your end?
But I won't back down; I will not bend.

Do you think, "Could I have saved him?"
You'll never know; you blew him off on a whim.

Don't turn around; you may hear him follow.
For its peace for ME he's looking to swallow.

For peace I don't have; I want him back.
Lessons for you? Add one more to your stack.

FUCK YOU

How the fuck do you look in the mirror?
Are you listening? Right now YOU'RE the hearer.

What kind of parents do you think you are?
He wanted to be loved, but you were too far.

I hate your mother fuckin' ways.

Your first son you killed because he was gay.

Lee wanted only to be loved by you.
You fucked him up! What did you do?

I will hate you till the day that I die.
You took him from me, and now I cry.

How do you feel? What's in your heart?
He was amazing, loving, giving, and smart.

You have to feel as parents you've failed.
On your heads the fate of them will be hailed.

He is gone from me and I blame you!
You're wicked, your ugly, you're sick like the flu!

But you don't care; he's out of your way.
He can't ask you for nothing; he doesn't have a say.

We'll I'll tell you what I have to say!
You're a fucker and a bitch; stay out of my way!

Don't try to blame me, and say I drove him.
He knows from me I only loved, cherished, and adored
him.

I shed tears every day for an incredible man.
How about you? Do you even remember him? Where do
you stand?

I should feel sadness for you, you know?
Do you even know love? How is it you show?

I say you haven't a clue.
I don't think you've even been blue.

So, pity for you is all you'll get from me.
Fuck pity, I hate you, for YOU are who took him from me.

From Tina

As if this were not enough; because I had been gone and was an emotional wreck, I was fired from my job (again), and as I mentioned, my dog was arrested. Yes, my dog, who at the time was my only sanity, was not a favorite of the neighbors. In fact, none of us were. We lived across the street from the former mayor of the city and his elderly mother lived right next door. Not only were we Californians with teenagers and a barking dog, but also a crazy mom. Not exactly desirable neighbors, but we did give them something to talk about. Hoss (my St. Bernard) had been barking; it was quite a racket coming from a two-hundred-pound dog. It was such a racket that the neighbors had him taken into custody. So, before I was actually released from the hospital, I went before the judge in order for him to decide my fate, as well as Hoss's.

My mother had flown up to take care of me and my mess of a life. She was horrified to see her daughter taken out of a police car in shackles, flanked by two officers, and escorted into the courtroom. The judge looked at me with pure bewilderment in his eyes. He showed some sympathy for me by releasing my dog, but the issue of my own future was still at stake. He wanted to put me in the state psychiatric institution because of my cutting. Going to the state hospital meant being put away for a very long time. This was a sobering thought. My cutting had gotten so bad that they were afraid that I could accidentally kill myself. Cutters don't generally use cutting as a form of suicide, but they have been known to kill themselves accidentally by cutting too deep; as could have been my case with the severity of my cuts.

Fortunately for me that day, the judge saw fit to release me into the custody of my mother; I was very thankful she was there. If she had not been, I would certainly have gone to the state hospital. From then on, my mother has been my salvation more times than I can count, and she continues to be. Actually, both of my parents are. Without my parents, I would never have made it through the things that I have had to face. These poems are chronologically out of order, but I'd like to share them now to show how important my parents have been to me during this journey I have been on. My parents are a gift and my lifeline.

MOTHER'S DAY

Why is it that you love me so?
I have done so many things as you've watched me grow.

So many choices that I did not know,
But you stuck by me even though.

I was a surprise as I came into your life,
But you put up with me even in strife.
To dad you were always the perfect wife.

I would count you one if there were such a thing as saints,

Because from me you will hear no complaints.

All miracles you have been to me.
Look behind you, and you too will see.
Your timeless joy has always lifted me.

What does your face look like without a smile?
You can see your face glow from as far as a mile,
Even through every trial.

There is so much I have put you through,
And the gifts you have given have not been few.
To you, every day brings something new.

A burden I may be still,
But caring for me has always been your will.
No matter that the walk is always up hill.

Mother's Day is here, and I want you to know,
I will hold on to you and never let you go.
Even when you're gone, I have learned to always grow.

FATHER'S DAY

How can there be a dad so strong,
That in his daughter's eyes he can do no wrong?
He has stood by her as the days grew long.

Each white hair on his head tells a story,
But to its end there was always glory.

Once a year is not enough to mark his day.
But for me on this day, I will never stray;

Because for me it marks each year that I will follow in his way.

Where would I be without his path to follow?
The world I know would pick me up and swallow;
In its ugly depths I would wallow.

Mistakes I've made, but he was always there
To pick up the pieces, and there was always enough to
share.
Sometimes I wonder why he would even care.

But love me he does in every way.
I know by my side he will always stay,
For the rest of my life each and every way.

He must know each and every night that I go to sleep
That my love for him is very deep.

I want to say that in every way
I wish him a Happy Father's Day.

To end my story about Lee, I will share this final poem. It was my poem of closure; my final days of staying stagnant in my grief. This poem also was one of many that have been published, and it won an editor's choice award.

THANK YOU

Thank you for letting me go,
Although the hurting is still so,

My new life will continue to grow.

You have given me your blessing.
In the distance, I can still hear you sing.
An angel you are; go ahead, and stretch those wings.

At peace now you are.
You'll always be near me, never far.
My protecting angel, I know you are.

Someday we will meet again in the sky.
Someday there will be no why.
Someday I will know the answer of why you died.

In my heart, you will always have a part.
Thank you for letting me have this new start.

In heaven, I feel you are looking down at me.
Growing and learning and moving on is what you will see.
For at peace is what I know you want me to be.

You have left me in this life never to return.
I ached so much my insides would burn.
In no other I could ever learn to turn.

You have given me something new to say good-bye.
I will miss you with all my heart, but this I will try.
Touch my face, turn and go, and I too will say good-bye.

CHAPTER 2
Stop Signs

Just when I thought I couldn't get kicked any harder, my ex-husband, Gene, had another surprise for me. While I was in the hospital, and all this with Lee and my possible sentence to the state hospital was going on, Gene filed papers to take custody of our children away from me. Of course, he got it. He had me proven as an unfit mother, and my legal rights to my children were taken. That was a mortally crushing blow. It was something I could not comprehend. My children were not *legally* mine anymore? What exactly did that mean? I didn't understand; I gave birth to these children, they are a part of my body, I have cared for them since that day. They are mine; what do you mean you are taking them from me? I have never had so much contempt and pure, hot anger at someone in my life; especially toward the one person whom I had loved so much. How could he have done this to me? Of course, looking back now, I completely understand why he did what he did. I was a mess! My babies did not need to see their mother like this. It was terribly traumatizing for them, and it will affect them for the rest of their lives. At the time, though, I could not imagine that one more thing was being taken from me, and that my life had been reduced to this point. What was happening to me? My children were about twelve, fourteen, and sixteen by now, so they could see me if they wanted to; he did not take away my physical custody, but the ultimate reality of the situation was the same.

Unfortunately, this began a horrendous stream of cutting. I had so much torment in me that it was unbearable, and cutting seemed to release so much of the emotion that was screaming to explode out of me. It was a temporary fix, of course, and in the long run, it only made matters worse, but I had no control over it whatsoever. At a certain point, I was going to my doctor almost daily for stitches. My family practice doctor would stitch me up without calling the authorities, which they are usually required to do. I think he genuinely felt sorry for me, but didn't know what he could do. Yet, he knew that if I did not come to him, I would be stitching them up myself. I would use a needle and thread from my sewing basket, and I took no care in the preparation or sterilization of my instruments; I just grabbed a needle and some thread and sewed them up. Surprisingly, I have never had an infection in any of my wounds. There was no pain, because there is a huge dump of adrenalin into your system, and it lasts a little while; long enough to stitch up the wound. I have even gone to the hospital and had the doctor stitch me up without any anesthesia. But, of course, once the adrenalin wears off, it is just like any other wound; it hurts! Caring for them is just like anything else, and I was always caring for a fresh cut in those days. The poems here describe some of my feelings about my cutting. The one titled, "My Empty Heart," was published and won an award also. These poems depict a very good description of my feelings about cutting.

THE DANCE

It lurks in the corners; it's haunting me.
The dark must flow to set me free.
How much more darkness does there need to be?

It's flowing from my veins again.
The pain is unbearable from within.
Why must it be? Is it my sin?

The edge of the blade calls my name.
My mind goes blank. Who is to blame?
It doesn't matter; it will flow all the same.

The dark, it runs; it makes a line.
My heart is stone; the line is fine.
You won't hear a sound; I will not whine.

The pain inside; why must it be?
What can I do to make it flee?
No one is there; they cannot see.

The lines there, they spell my pain.
But what from the dark is there to gain?
It's dark as crimson; it leaves a stain.

Find my blade, razor sharp to touch.
Cut out the pain; it is too much
It is killing me; the pain is such.

I cannot stop; it's controlling me.
From this addiction, I want to flee.
What is my life? Where will it be?

Take the razors; take them all.
Hold me down; don't let me fall.
What is your name? Who do I call?

I try to hide; it's chasing me.
The darkness is calling; will it beat me?
Someone look; won't someone see?

Can't you read between the lines?
You know they are there, but they are mine.
Don't look; don't see me cry this time.

I walk to it as if in a trance,
For with the blade, it becomes a lance.
The darkness and me, we will do our dance.

INSIDE MYSELF

I'm looking inside myself; who is there?
How deep do I go? Do I dare?
I close my eyes; the feelings can I spare?

There're trying to break the surface I feel.
Will they make it? Will they break the seal?
Is what's down there, is it real?

The higher it gets, the more it hurts me.
I don't want to feel it, don't you see?
Just push it away; I want to be free.

The pain I've had has been so long.
I close it off; is it so wrong?
The feelings I have, you can hear them in a song.

The pushing up feels like an explosion.
Get away; I just want to run.

The blade is my savior; it takes it away.
With that cut, it will not stay.
Gone again, though it's sad to say.

Inside myself I don't want to see.
Do you understand? Will you let me be?
Just leave it all alone; will you just agree?

I know my body; destroyed it's become.
The pain is so strong; it rises and it hums.
Add it all up; you can't find the sum.

Quiet you hear, but inside is a war.
The meds they give me, what are they for?
All they do is help close the door.

I am beyond fixing; this is true.
What would you do if this was you?
Could you handle the agony that's not little or few?

So let me be; just walk away.
I can't ask you to deal with me and stay.
I wish I could; I wish there were a way.

MY EMPTY HEART

Where in this life is my place?
I feel that I no longer have a face.
The world flashes by me as if it's in a race.

I feel like there is wave after wave of sadness.
Is it real? Or is it just my madness?

My insides, they are so weak and fragile.
Can I stop it? Or is it all against my will?
My empty heart, I wish there was something to fill.

I look around and dizziness is all I get.
Why is it I can't seem to forget?
Is this all it is? Is my life set?

The colors, they blend as a washed-out painting.
I am so tired of wanting and waiting.
Where am I going? What is this time creating?

My life, it's a grave, no life remaining.
My headstone, it is blank; the vision is fading.

Peace and love is what I long for.
It hurts from my depth, my inner core.
But I feel like a wound, an unhealing sore.

I look at my scars, and remember each one.
Why can't I feel the warmth of the sun?
I want to hide, but when it changes I run.
There's something against my head, a loaded gun.

I'm walking through life looking, not finding.
It won't go farther; just keeps rewinding.
Where is my cloud with that silver lining?

Someone reach out; pull me close.
Don't let go, or so the song goes.
Each time I sniff, I can't smell that rose.

My head, it is full; it's confused and its lost.
My heart it is broken, but at what cost?
But alone I stand, cold as the frost.

Empty again, I feel today.
Where do I go? Tell me which way.
Open my mouth; what will I say?

Will my heart always feel as empty and hollow?
All I want is someone to follow.
My throat it is tight; I can hardly swallow.

Is someone to love me too much to ask?
Someone to share life in the sun, just lay and bask.
Or will he too be taken, as I hide behind my mask.

I don't want to go through this life alone.
What happened to my years? I thought I had grown.
But my life, it's behind me, nothing to be shown.

I'll go on in this life because I have to.
But life and love, today there is nothing.

My kids took a huge hit from the symptoms of my illness. Jake, in particular, saw way too much. He was the one who was around the most because he was my caretaker. He thought he could save me. He tried so hard to take care of me. I cry as I write this. He was the little boy who offered his mom ice cream when she was having a bad day, because ice cream fixed everything. Jake is the most sensitive of the three children; he is like his dad. He rarely talks to me now, and the burden that I carry for that is excruciatingly heavy and painful. I try so hard to make up for it, but nothing seems to work; I can only hope that someday he will come back to me.

Sarah has abandonment issues because she feels like I emotionally checked out during a very difficult period for her, and we had been extremely close. Fortunately, she is the oldest and has been able to work through a lot of her anger and pain, and we have been able to rebuild our relationship after a time when she didn't speak to me for nearly two years.

My youngest son Daniel still struggles with the past in a way that he won't talk about, but he does understand the illness that I was a victim of and the reasons I did the things I did.

The following are two poems. The first one I wrote to Jake, and the second one I wrote to Daniel. I have written many poems to all my children; all expressions of the immense amount of love I have for them and the need of their forgiveness.

MY HEARTBEAT

Why it is that life takes so much away?
Who are the ones that will go, and who will stay?
Sometimes we wonder why we have to face another day.

I think of you, and I see your child's face.
But the man is there now; it has taken the child's place.

You used to look to me with trust and love in your eyes.
Now your eyes, they are covered in a disguise.

The things life has brought us has hardened you.
I hurt for us and don't know what to do.

You and me, we were a team.
Indestructible, inseparable is what it seemed.

I long for the day you will give me that back,
Cause without you the darkness in my heart is black.

I tell myself; someday, someday…
But that keeps getting harder and harder to say.

Do you ever think about how much I love you?
Or are those thoughts so very few?

Should I list for you all the amazing things you are?
Or maybe, you just being my son is good enough so far?
Because to me, my son, my simple man is what you are.

Happiness is what I want you to find,
Contentment, too, and peace of mind.

Maybe someday you will include me.
That would give me happiness and peace of mind to be.

Just know that I will never go away.
I am your mom; I am here to stay.

Wherever I am, my blood runs in your veins.
And you are part of my heartbeat; we are linked like
chains.

I love you like no mother can,
Since you're first breath ... since your life began.

YOU NEED TO KNOW

I remember when your hand in mine was all you could
need.
Now you're scared that I sometimes bleed.

You are so strong; I can see it in your eye.
To know that you have to be makes me cry.
I look at our lives and always ask why.

You deserve so much better than I can give.
Look at this life that you must live.

I want you to be happy as you should be.
I live with shame and guilt for that; don't you see?

I love you more than you could ever know,
Each and every moment as I've watched you grow.

The life I've lived has not been an easy one,
But I am sad for the pain it has caused my son.
If only it could be rewound and undone.

I'd take back every scar I have left on your heart,
Open you up and take you apart.
Go back and make a new start.

I hope for me you will find forgiveness,
Understanding, and love, though I don't deserve this.

As you grow older, maybe you will have peace.
Of all the anger and hurt you will find release.

For me I give no mercy or grace;
For my children are far bigger than time or space.

I have so much guilt for the seeds I've sown,
So much pain for the hurt you have known.
But I promise I will never leave you alone.

Never leave me; I need you so.
It scares me as I see you grow.
I love you so much, you need to know.

I wrote a poem entitled "Friend?" It was not a very nice poem, as you will see when you read it. I wrote it during a very particular paranoid stage I was going through. I have a very good friend, Suzanne. She and her husband Jim were our very best friends; in fact, they moved to Idaho shortly after we did. Our families were extremely close. We did everything together. Our kids were similar in ages, and we all had like interests that we shared. It was very hard on Suzanne to watch me go through my breakdown. She did not understand what was happening to her best friend. To her credit, she went out and researched bipolar disorder to try and figure out what was going on with me and where her friend had disappeared to. She stood by me even when I lied right to her face, which was on many occasions. She was still always there for me, and so was Jim.

Then one night my kids were going to spend the night at her house. (She lived just a few blocks away.) I had been going out almost every night but was coming home at a reasonable hour because I had the kids at home with me alone. Gene was still living away from the house. This particular night, I decided to stay out late since the kids were at Suzanne's house. I came home at about two in the morning and found a note on the door that said Jake wanted to come home, so I drove over to Suzanne's house to get him. I knocked on the door. Suzanne came to the door and was angry at me because of the time and told me that she would not let Jake come home now because the kids were all asleep. When she proceeded to close the door, I got angry and told her that I wasn't leaving without Jake. She closed and locked the door. That was not a very good idea on Suzanne's part, because now I was very angry. I stood there and continued to relentlessly ring the doorbell. She called the police. Now the entire household was up. My kids were wondering what was going on, and everyone was upset. When the police got there and heard both of our stories, he told Suzanne that she could not keep my children from me, and he told me that I should just let things go for tonight; Suzanne and I could work out our differences in the morning. So I did just that; I left my kids there for the night, and then I forbid them to ever go over there again.

Hence, you have my poem on friendship. I felt betrayed because I did not understand why she was trying to keep my kids away from me. Yes, it was two in the morning, and I had been out. Okay, I was probably not being a very attentive mother, but I did not agree that it was her place to step in. Her side of the story was that she was protecting them. Considering all that was going on at the time, I see where she was coming from now; water under the bridge. Suzanne and I are still the very best of friends; in fact, I still consider her my best friend. I love her deeply and always will; we have been through hell together. There are scars that we share that will remain, but we have overcome some huge hurdles. So keep in mind when you read this poem that it was out of anger of feeling betrayed and my state of paranoia. The incident with Suzanne inspired this poem, but it is not particularly about her. At that time, I was feeling like *everyone* was against me, even my best friend.

FRIEND?

Don't try to be my friend.
You won't be there in the end,
And your reasons you cannot defend.

You don't understand; you do not try.
Don't you see I know it, and it makes me cry?
You look at me, and your face asks me why.

Just stay away from me.
Don't get close; I need to be free.
What is in my heart, you could never see.

Sometimes I reach out, and you're not there.
It doesn't surprise me that I don't know where.
The boundaries you set, they are not fair.

Here is my circle; don't cross that line.
Don't worry about me; I will be fine.
I do not need you; I will not whine.

Alone is what I can only be.
For everyone that tries, there is a fee.
I'm not paying it; I just need to be me.

Friends are selfish, thinking only of them.
So what is a friend, I ask you then?
I know, I've seen, I remember when.

Betrayal is all its about to be.
Just watch, open their mouths, you will see.
I will just close up; I will only flee.

Alone is better, but painful, I tell.
I do not want what they have to sell.
My heart I hide deep in a cold, dark well.

Just go your way; I do not need you.
I can manage; I know what to do.
If I can control it, the pains will be few.

You're on that side; I'm on mine.
Look the other way; I'll be fine.
My circle is drawn; don't cross that line.
All I know is what is mine.

As far as my illness goes, my cutting was by far the most difficult part for my family to deal with or to understand. It is very common for people who suffer with bipolar disorder to have an addiction of some sort. Drugs or alcohol are the most common, but others may include: gambling, spending large amounts of money, and sexual addiction. Because of the intense mood swings, emotions run very high, and there is a strong need for an outlet. Unfortunately, they come out in the forms of bad behavior or addictions; mine was cutting. That was my coping skill. It took me over five years to learn how to handle my emotions in other, healthier ways and to stop cutting. To date, it has been two and a half years with no cutting episodes. It was very hard for me to give up. I would feel such horrible fears and feelings inside me that I could not bear it. I call those intense fears and emotions that could bring me to my knees my "monster." The feelings can actually be physically painful. When I used my blade to cut, it felt like a huge release. All that pent-up pain would just fly out of me in a giant *whoosh*! Yes, it was temporary, and once the episode was over, I had to go get stitches. Then I would have to deal with the wounds and scars that would last a lifetime; but at the time, it was worth it. This poem and others talk about that monster.

THE MONSTER INSIDE

I scream inside,
But you can't hear me.
I make no sound.

I am running away.
I look over my shoulder,
But I don't turn around.

The monster inside is trembling.
It is starting to roar.
I try to force it back down.

All of this pain is tearing me up.
It's got its hands around my throat;
Keeping me from breathing,
Making me drown.

I cut my skin to release,
Release the monster inside;
But with each cut he drives deeper.

Why am I its host?
Why do I have to live this life?
Why do I have to be its keeper?

When will it leave me in peace?
I want to pull off my skin and hide.
But the monster only grows bigger.

My world is crumbling.
No one can see it I hide it;
But the finger is on the trigger.

No one knows the pain of the monster.
Its claws are deep.
It holds on tighter.

But I'll keep fighting to release it.
I'll not fall to its prey.
Tomorrow may be better; it may be alright.

I went through a deep depression at this time. Lee's death and my kids being taken away from me had all taken its toll. I had been very happy at my job. It was a very nice day spa in Boise, and I was doing very well there. I had built a considerably heavy clientele in the short amount of time I had been there, and I was one of the top retailers. I got along with everyone and even my boss liked me, which was a plus since she was a real hard nose. When I took flight to hide from Lee, I was gone a few days. Then I spent a few days in the hospital. Needless to say, when I came back to work, word had already gotten around. Now, I will let you draw your own conclusion on this, but here is what happened, and it is brief. My boss did not want to talk to me, and I am not even sure what story she heard, therefore I was not given any chance to plead my case. My mother was asked to come in and collect my things, I was fired immediately, and my boss did not want to see me at all, or ever again. End of story; I never went back. I guess I shouldn't have expected any other response, but you know what? I did! I thought she should have at least talked to me and heard what had happened; and if she wanted to fire me, she should have told me face to face after hearing me out.

At this point, I had to move out of my house. I had gotten the house in the divorce, and it was up for sale. We were in danger of losing it, and we were in the process of going bankrupt. I had to leave; being there was proving to make my depression even worse. I was just hiding in my bed most of the time. My mother once again came to take care of me.

By now, I was able to get permanent disability. My bipolar disorder was debilitating enough with the cutting to keep me from working. Employers frowned upon their employees bleeding on the job. Also, I was so emotionally ravaged that stress was a big enemy for me. I was so fragile that the slightest provocation to my mental state reverberated like an earthquake. I was literally hanging on the edge of sanity. It took me only a few weeks to begin receiving benefits from Social Security for permanent disability. It is usually a grueling process of being rejected and reapplying, often more than once; not so in my case.

We decided I would go to school at Boise State University

and take a class to keep me occupied and find a new direction for my life. We found a tiny little house for me to rent only a mile from the college. I could walk to school every day if I wanted to, *and* I could have my dog Hoss with me. It is hard to find a homeowner who will let you bring along your two-hundred-pound house pet.

I was still grieving heavily for Lee and feeling the loss of my children. My medications at this time were also very sedating, perhaps bringing me too low. I was feeling very lost and alone at this point of my journey; I was lost in deep depression, as my poems reflect.

I WANT TO DIE

Everything I see turns to gray in my eyes.
I see the dirt the dust of the street fly high.
I look around, nothing makes sense; I ask why.
What do I want? You ask of me. I want to die.

Lee is gone; he's an angel now.
I want to be with him; tell me how.
What I want no one will allow.

I hurt so deep; the depth is unknown.
What does this life have for me? What has it shown?
All I do is look around and feel so alone.

There is only one thing I feel, pain inside.
Just cut me up; open me wide.
I want so bad to get off this painful ride.

I want to be with Lee; let me somehow.
I need to go; no one needs me, and it shows.
I want to be part of the wind; let me blow.

I have agony inside me; no one knows or sees.
Look in my eyes; someone see, I beg you please.
It's too hard. Let the blood flow; soon it will ease.

The blade is there, calling my name.
Don't make me look at it and feel shame.
It's not you or me, no ones' to blame.

Lee is calling; he wants me too.
The days we had were way too few.
Just look at me; I'm a mess to view.

Blood everywhere, I'm slipping away.
Don't hold me back; don't make me stay.
Open wide the clouds; make my way.

No one understands; they think they do.
How can you? You're not me; I'm not you.
Just turn your back; don't look my way, take your cue.

I sit and I tremble and cry in sadness.
What do you think? Is it my madness?

What difference does it make?
Unlike Lee, will there be a wake?
I'm so sad and alone it makes me shake.
It would have been so much easier for him to take;
Taken me with him so we both could awake.

Why did I run? With him is where I belong.
I can hear him; he is calling me, singing my song.
Is what I want, is it really so wrong?

I was at Lori, my therapist's office one day. I was seeing her two or three times a week. On this day, I had a very bad headache. Along with my other meds, I had taken some prescription pain killers. While we talked, I started sneezing and my nose started running from my allergies acting up, so I took some Benadryl. This, of course, was on top of all the psychotropic drugs I was already taking. (One of which I was NOT supposed to take Benadryl with.) Not one of the smartest things I ever did. I began to get very sleepy toward the end of our session. By the time we were done, I was not just *a little* sleepy, I was ridiculously sleepy! She asked me to stay for a few minutes and not drive home yet, so I sat on the couch in her office to wait for it to wear off. It didn't. The next thing I knew, I was lying on a bed in the emergency room being yelled at by a nurse to drink a very large cup of black charcoal. I was very foggy-headed to say the least, and I had no idea whatsoever how I had gotten there; I *did* understand that if I didn't drink the charcoal, they were going to shove a tube down my throat. I had overdosed myself. If I had been alone, I easily could have died. It was my first realization that prescription drugs are not to be underestimated. I drank the charcoal.

It took over two years, and approximately 20 different medication trials to get to a point where we found a combination that was beginning to show an improvement. There are so many possible drug combinations, and every person is different. It takes months and even years to find the right combination that is most effective for each individual's symptoms. Unfortunately, this proves to be more than many with bipolar can handle. It takes much courage, patience, and persistence to find the right combination, and because people with bipolar disorder generally enjoy the highs, they find it uncomfortable to come down to what would be considered a normal level (if normal can be defined, that is).

Many of them also do not like the feeling of being sedated (though that is a side effect that can usually be dealt with, or can wear off after your body adjusts to the medication). The perfect concoction would be that which would keep one's mood in an area that keeps them from going too high or too low. It took me nearly three years of tweaking and adjusting to find that perfect fit, and adjustments still need to be made here and there depending on what is going on in life. Stress in particular can require an adjustment because of added anxiety.

School was great; I loved it. I took an English/writing class the first semester. I earned an A and was extremely proud of myself. I felt like I was getting a grip again. Even my poems had at least some glimmer of hope in them. This one is actually one of my favorites.

CLOSE THE DOOR

Open my heart; spill it on the ground.
Catch what you will, yet you won't hear a sound.

Am I still breathing? Feel my chest fall.
Its cold, it's solid, like a high brick wall.
Are you there? Can you hear me when I call?

The past, it has taken so much of me.
I fight and I cry, but it won't let me be.
Look deep in my eyes, is there something to see?

Why does the past take and never give back?
It takes and it keeps; it hoards its stack.

I reach back into the dark, yet nothing I feel.
Can't someone turn it, reverse that wheel?
The door won't open; it's frozen in steel.

But time moves forward; it will know.
It knows what the past will not show.
Time is a river; just let it flow.

The past and today, they too will meet.
Like the sun and the soil in the day's heat.
It all moves together like a field of wheat.

So don't mourn for what is gone and past,
Because a day like today, it will not last.

My breathing chest will continue to fall.
This I know, but that's not all.

The pain of my past, it will not win.
I'm on new ground, a river to swim in.
The past has taken with it all of my sin.

I won't be afraid of what is gone,
And I will not fear the rise of the dawn.
I guess I will stay on this ride that I'm on.

Close the door to the past, open the new.
Take each new day like there are only a few.

Other than my room, I had another place that I liked to
escape too, and I wrote about it a couple of times. One of the

biggest attractions about Idaho for me was the mountains and the rivers. I have always been more of a mountain girl than a beach girl; unusual I guess for a girl who is Southern California homegrown. So when I wanted an escape, I would head for the mountains (which was a mere fifteen-minute drive) and to some of my favorite spots: the hot springs. I knew where a few of them were; exploring them was something I loved to do. I would get right down to the bare essentials and soak for hours. Rain or shine, it didn't matter. Some of my best times were when it was raining outside and the steam was thick like fog, emanating off the rock as the hot water just poured down the side of the cliff into the pool I was lying in. On one of these wondrously, serene days, I was lying on the edge of a cliff in a pool about a hundred feet over the river. It was raining, and all I could hear was the pitter patter of the drops on the hot, steamy water I was soaking in and the rushing of the river below. The mist was heavy as it mixed with the fog on this cold day in late fall. It felt as though there were clouds floating all around me, and I was in the middle of a fairytale story; all was quiet. Suddenly, a beautiful bald eagle burst from the misty fog and flew right past me through the canyon, his wings stretched wide and proud; it was mesmerizing. I can still hear his screeching call as he flew past. It is a scene that runs clear in my mind that I won't ever forget. I know that in my mind's eye I can always go back to that moment. Memories like that can never be taken away.

PEACE

So much peace is hard to find.
There is little escape from my mind.
Why is it so hard to unwind?
So much baggage I want to leave behind.

The sky is cloudy; my heart is gray.
I sit and I listen with nothing to say.
Right now there is nothing in my way.
Right now everything seems okay.

So much peace I feel around me.
So much life and beauty that I see.
Is it possible? Can it be
That the peace that I see is inside of me?

My body, it floats; all my muscles relaxed.
My eyes, they are closed; even my mind is relaxed.

The sky I can touch.
I've missed this so much.

All this is here, not far away.
My escape, it is close; I want to stay.
Take all the hurt and throw it away.
So much to express, I can't even say.

Feel the heat outside my skin.
The steam, it is cleansing from within.
The river, it winds taking away my sin.
While I am here, I feel I can win.

The coldness of the world is far away.
I want it to stay and keep it at bay.

The feel of the rock is under my skin.
It is strong and holding me, keeping me in.

The river it, winds far below.
Good things are to come, of this I know.
The mountains they tell me, just take it slow.

Please don't make me leave this place.
Can you see the peace that is on my face?
This time that I have, don't let me waste.
I want to take it with me, not leave it in haste.

At least I know there is such a refuge to go.
Look up to the mountains, I can still see and know.
It will always be there, of this I know.
Remember the high, run away from the low.

I can run and hide away to this place,
When things are hard, I don't want to face.
Bad feelings inside I want to erase.
Look up to the sky; let it soothe my face.

THE RIVER'S EDGE

I step closer to the edge.
I look down and see the water rushing by.
My toes are hanging now over the ledge.

I throw my head back, eyes closed,
My arms outstretched.
I breathe deep and long through my nose.

Where do I go from here?
My life is a burden I no longer want to carry.
Along with the burden, there is great fear.

I look to the river below,
Strong and powerful with purpose and strength.
Why can't I have that? Does someone know?

If I jump to its depths, will I become a part of it,
Washing away all my sorrow?
Or will it deceive me, and thrash me when I hit?

I want to BE that river there below.
No care in the world,
Its only need is to flow.

Nothing stops it; nothing gets in its way.
It is all powerful between the canyon walls.
This is the place that I want to stay.

The mist that rises from the crashing waves,
It dampens my skin.
A gift that says the water will save.

I lean out over as far as I can.
I want to jump; I want to be a part of this beautiful thing,
But I look behind me, and I see a man.

He is standing in the mist and calling my name.
I can see his lips move though there is no sound,
But his voice makes me feel shame.

The look on his face is agony.
He is stretching his hand out to come to him,
Yet the mist is thick as honey.

I look once more at the river below.
I feel I am betraying my destiny,
But I turn and I take the hand that I know.

This man I love is stronger than the river's ache.
Though there is a hole in my heart for the river,
Trusting him must be no mistake.

Yet, someday to the river I must return,
For here there is no fear.
This is my true destiny, and here is where I will return.

I was to meet a new man about this time on my journey. His name was Ray. We met on the Internet, talked for a while, and soon met up in person for coffee at Starbucks. It was three hours of grilling each other. We covered every taboo subject from politics to religion to abortion and same sex marriage. What we found was that we liked each other very much, though it began the most turbulent, chaotic relationship of my life.

Sometimes having everything in common is a great thing; sometimes it is not. As for Ray and me, it was not. Yes, we got along very well for the most part because we liked similar pleasures in life, such as music, movies, and motocross (he got me involved in riding while we were together). We also had equal values and ethics. But Ray also had some mental disturbances like me. I was still trying to deal with my bipolar disorder by tweaking medications every time I turned around and seeing Lori two or more times a week. The process was grueling, because my moods would fluctuate terribly as the medication sent my brain off in all directions as it tried to get control. It was hard for me to live with *me* sometimes. Ray had obsessive compulsive disorder (OCD) and chronic depression. He had lost his mother to a long-term illness four years prior and had been devastated by it; he had not fully recovered. His depression was sometimes debilitating for him, and to make matters worse, his OCD caused him to be anorexic. He was obsessive about his weight and his body. But it was his depression that was the hardest; he would cry most every night at times, and I could not help him. This sometimes sent me into a tailspin of my own, because the stress of dealing with him would trigger my own symptoms. I had a terrible fear of being abandoned at that time, and paranoia was still a problem for me.

My relationship with Ray was extremely erratic and off and on. One minute we were as happy as we could be, and the next, he was moving out and leaving me to go back to Las Vegas where his family was. Interestingly, I wrote many poems about Ray (more than I have here), but I threw a lot of them away. Most of the ones I did write were usually beseeching him to be strong and keep going. He referred to suicide often, which of course scared the hell out of me after what I had already been through with Lee. I could not go through that again.

The first poem is referring to the new changes in my life again; the others are about Ray.

TOMORROW

Tomorrow seems to creep up on you.
What you see behind you is anything but few.

Does thought change your way?
What would it take to stop and stay?

Tomorrow is uncertain; it causes fear.
Keep your mind open; it must be clear.

Can I trust myself? Is my mind well?
Sometimes it's the wind blowing through a hollow shell.

Each corner I take, my fear grows great.
What will be there? What is my fate?

Nothing in life is certain; promises can be broken.
I'm on a roller coaster, my hands full of tokens.

I'm afraid to get off, to have my feet on the ground.
Sometimes I listen; there is no sound.

Forgiveness for myself is hard to find.
Sometimes I wish I could just rewind.

The blood of my life pulses through my veins.
But tomorrow it seems, has something to gain.

BE SURE OF YOUR LIGHT

You're lost in your head; I can't find you.
Where did you go? What is left is so few.
Please let me open you up and break through.

The pain you have is destroying you now.
I don't know where you can hide; I don't know how.
Why do you let it? Why do you allow?

The pain inside me is a knife through my heart.
I want to be with you always, not apart.
Can't we start over, make a new start?

Your spirit is rising; I know what you seek.
Your defenses are falling; you are growing weak.

That place is far; your turn is not today.
Who are you to judge in which way?
Don't you dare leave me; you must stay.

Grow strong again; I know you can.
We can do it together; we can stand.

Know yourself; be sure of your light.
Where are you going? Look ahead and fight.
Try and try with all your might.

The darkness is far; it is not near you.
Don't fear it; it can't harm you. It's only a view.
Love from above is watching out, too.

The pit is cold and dark and deep.
Look and your feet; they are starting to seep.
My heart is crying out; I am beginning to weep.

I know you can make it; just find a way how.
Do it fast; do it now!
I am here; come to me somehow.

Open your skin; step out into the new.
Don't look back; its dissolving like the dew.
You are strong and able; go on and be you.

POISON

My blood ran pure, as did yours.
They were together, a strong force.

Now a poison has invaded our veins.
The poison is causing great pain.

I take the blade, expel the poison.
It's the only way, though deeply unspoken.

The bleeding is not working; cut again.
I must do it to save this man.

The man I loved has been taken away.
Whether he'll come back to me I cannot say.

The poison I put there, and my heart breaks.
Cut again and again, for my heart aches.

His blood and mine must run pure again.
Things must be beautiful and happy as it began.

Removing the poison is the only way.
I will conquer it; I will not let it stay.

I will cut and let the poison go away.
He will love me again someday.

PROMISE

A promise is strong; it stands true.
Some can make it, but there are few.
A promise is not old; it is always new.

What you feel for me, is it real?
Take my hand in yours; it will seal.
Till death us part; that's the deal.

Look in my eyes; are they old?
Together we'll be till our bones are cold
We will stand, we will not fold.

My life is yours, and yours is mine.
Never will either of us cross that line.
It will only grow better as a bottle of wine.

That promise to me, can you make?
All of you is what I'll take.
My promise to you I will not fake.

When most break promises, ours will stand.
Never let go; hold tight my hand.
This high we have, it will not land.

I love you with all my heart.
Our life is a painting, a piece of art.
Our promises are made to never part.
This is our beginning, a beautiful start.

I actually wrote very few poems in 2006; maybe less than ten the whole year. I also have a lot of memory loss from the two years I was with Ray. I actually have to ask my mother about certain parts of this section of my life; and when reminded, sometimes it still doesn't bring the memory back to the surface. It is like there are chunks of my life that are gone forever. Memory loss is a funny thing, and it can be very frustrating and also very frightening. I am plagued with giant black holes of memory loss during those difficult years between 2003 and 2006, and even parts of 2007. And due to my early sexual abuse, most of my childhood memory is also missing. Unfortunately, I also have to deal with short-term memory loss due to side effects of medication. Yet, I feel that sometimes the brain has mercy on us; it hides some of the painful things that may cause us unrelenting agony. And for that, except for occasional flashbacks, I will be grateful.

While Ray and I were together, my cutting continued and began to worry my family and my doctors. My doctors suggested that I check into a hospital in Washington to seek further treatment. It was at a place called Lake Chalan. I actually have no memory of this place at all. I only have a few journal entries from the near three weeks I spent there. I could not even describe any part of that hospital; it has been completely wiped from my memory.

It was an expensive visit, but I believe it helped to a degree at the time. However, it did not leave a lasting impression. I think my head was so cloudy from stress and medications, and my brain was still so unbalanced. I was still not able to get enough relief.

Here is where I made a very crucial, horrendous mistake in my life that I wish I could go back and change. I left Idaho to move to Las Vegas with Ray. He wanted to pursue a job that he was offered there. He had become discontent with the job that he had in Boise, even though it had been a very good one. Unfortunately, the man who was giving him the job made a lot of very false promises, and the job did not end up being what is was supposed to be. We were only there six months, but in the meantime, I had left Sarah and Jacob with their dad and Daniel had come with Ray and me. I had no idea at the time of the effect that my leaving would have on my two children I was leaving behind. Now I understand the effect that it had on them at the ages they were, but at the time I felt they didn't need me anymore. Now I know they did.

I almost feel like this book is a memoir of my regrets. In a way, I guess it is. Mental illness is so misunderstood. I hate to use the word "victim," but that truly is what you are when you are the host of a mental disease. It is just like any other illness, diabetes, heart disease, cancer, etc. You don't have a choice; you can't take vitamins to try to prevent it, you can't take an antibiotic to get rid of it, and you certainly can't just let it run its course. You have to *live with it* every single day. Like other diseases, you can manage it to the best of your ability and with as much knowledge as science has come up with to this point, but the fact remains that you *will* live with it. During the course of our day, we generally don't think about checking ourselves and questioning what our brain tells us to do. We just do what we do, right? Well, what if you were afraid of your brain; never knowing if you could fully trust that it was giving you correct information? Am I acting right? Did I just say something really stupid or weird? Does that person know I have a mental illness? Did I make the right decision? Because if you didn't, you know you will be paying for it later, and in the worst case scenario, for the rest of your life. Can you imagine the fear of living with an illness that affects the primary organ of your body that controls every aspect of everything that you do every minute of every day? The fear of never being able to trust what controls how you act, what you say and how you think? It's a fear unlike any other.

PAINT ME BLACK

What is wrong with me?
What is it that I don't see?

I look in the mirror, and who stares back?
Am I a monster? Maybe the mirror will crack.
Blot out my face; just paint me black.

My heart beats; I feel it in my chest.
My intentions are true; I do my best.

I don't mean to hurt you.
To love all is what I want to do.

I'm walking a tightrope; the earth is far below.
I shake and tremble as the wind begins to blow.
Will someone be there if I fall? Of this, I don't know.

Sometimes I feel far away and alone,
Separated by a wall of stone.

Words cut me and make me bleed;
On my weakness words feed.
Mean words are painful and full of greed.

Do you see the light in my eyes grow dim?
In their brightness is where you would swim.

Under the cover of pretension is where I will hide.
It is safe there; that is where I will reside.

Everyone takes, and few give back.
What is it they find that I lack?

My soul is full of love with no end;
Unconditionally to each, I will send
But if you can't give it back, don't pretend.

I guess I will walk alone with my madness or insanity.
But look at you with all your profanity.

It is easy for you to judge me.
My scars are out there for all to see.

But if we could see yours, where would they be?
You too might be a host of a little madness; won't you
agree?
So take the knife from my back; just let me be.

I will close my door and not let you in.
If your intention is to hurt me, you won't win.
I will just turn my back and begin again.

Life with Ray was crazy. We were on, and we were off; back
and forth all the time. This wreaked havoc with my illness.
Every day was like a rollercoaster ride. We were what you
call a codependent relationship. With my bipolar disorder
and his depression/OCD, we were one big mess. We fed off
of each other like two hungry animals.

I can remember one time we broke up, and he was going
to be leaving to go back to Las Vegas. I was extremely upset.
It was during those days when I had no capacity to deal with
my emotions, and cutting was my solution. I had no blades
in the house; I believe he had removed them. I had always

had blades tucked away in places where I knew I could get them. They were like security blankets to me. I never really used knifes or other sharp instruments; they had to be razor blades. Since I was a hairdresser, I preferred straight blades used in barbering; although if these were not available, I would use what was at hand. But on this day, I drove to the store to go get a new blade. I can't say why, because I don't particularly like alcohol and I rarely drink, but I also bought a bottle of wine. I was gone awhile and Ray was worried about me, so he called the police. They were waiting for me when I got back home.

It is important to understand something about the police. I can only understand this now because my boyfriend Jimmy is a retired police officer of the NYPD, and he has taught me many things. The police have to always be prepared to handle the situation by keeping everyone involved safe according to the worst-case scenario. By Ray's word, they already knew I was a danger to myself, so this put them in high-alert status right away. I was unprepared for what was coming when I drove down my street and pulled into the driveway.

There were two police cars and four officers standing in my yard. When I got out, the bag in my hand, which carried a brand new blade and a bottle of wine, was immediately taken from me. I was then placed up against a police car and patted down for other weapons. As I was being cuffed in front of my very curious neighbors, I was, in a not so ladylike way, telling Ray that I was never going to forgive him for *this one*. About then was when I was tucked away into the backseat of the police car, and I was once again taken to the psychiatric hospital.

There did come a point when Ray and I separated for a short time. That was when he was offered his job in Henderson, Nevada. Ray was going to go on ahead and get us settled, and I was going to go to stay at my sister's house in California. My mom flew out (again) to help me drive from Idaho to California with a U-Haul truck, my car, my pug, my St. Bernard, and all my belongings. Nothing is ever easy, is it? First of all, I was extremely distressed at being separated from Ray for an undefined amount of time, and I wasn't too happy about going to California either, though my family thought it was the best solution for me. After all I had been through, I had given up a lot of my independence. There were two main reasons. The first was that I was scared to death to make any decisions, based on my current decision-making skills. In other words, I was scared to death of myself. I couldn't trust my brain. Looking back now, I was right. The other reason was that I was so incapacitated by my illness and my lack of proper decision-making skills, that I was almost childlike and needed to be guided. This is what I was reduced to from an extremely strong woman who was a wife, ran a house, raised four children, and ran a full-time business. The reality of my life was crippling.

Ray left, with a teary departure, and shortly thereafter, my mom and I drove away from my little home in Boise back to California. It would be approximately one thousand miles, and we would stop and sleep in a motel about half way. I drove my car; an eighties-something model Lincoln, and my mom followed me in the U-Haul truck. We had one little worry: I would get very sleepy while driving because of my medications. I thought I had it covered though, because I had my music to listen to, and I also had both my dogs in the car with me to keep me company. A two–hundred-pound St. Bernard sitting next to you is a pretty good distraction. Yet, it wasn't enough. I began to drift off. My car veered across the two-lane highway and dipped into the ditch on the other side. This must have awakened me, because I came back onto the highway, crossed, and went into the ditch on the other side. I was traveling at a high rate of speed, so still dazed, I went back across the highway again and stopped on the other shoulder facing traffic. Fortunately, there had been no cars on that stretch of highway at that particular moment, only my mother, who watched this whole scene from behind in terror. As she came to the side of the car to see if I was okay, we were in for a surprise. Hoss, was very tightly wedged between the driver's seat and the driver's door! Completely stumped by how this happened, it took us a while to work an extremely traumatized dog out of that position. If that were not enough, poor little Candy, my pug, was extremely distraught as she lay in her crate which was upside down on the floor of the back seat.

Now in high, triple-digit heat, we all piled into the U-Haul and proceeded on our way. Later, the tow truck company told us that all the rubber on my tires had been completely peeled back off the rims. If I had been in a small car, and not my big "boat," my car would have flipped and things could have been much worse. Once again, it was not my time to leave this earth.

I made it to my sister's house, where I spent a few weeks. My sister was still having a terribly hard time seeing me in my state of complete mental anguish. I just wasn't the same person anymore. I had always been the stronger, older sister, so upbeat, crazy, happy … insane! Everyone was used to the manic Tina, because that is what I was most of the time. Up until I hit my breaking point that is. Then my mania went through the roof, and I would sink into depression. I had a strange vulnerability about me now; my strength was gone.

So I had a brief reprieve from the madness with Ray, hiding away in my sister's guest house. At this time, my son Daniel was not with me, but he would catch up with us later in Nevada. For the time being, until I was summoned by Ray, everyone just tried to keep me busy with the secret hope that I would not be returning to Ray's side, but my mind was set. I should have listened.

Things were crazy with Ray, but we managed to stay together for two years. When we left Idaho and moved to Henderson, Nevada, the job he took was not what it was supposed to be, and he was miserable. He went on the hunt for another one. He found one in South Carolina. If my family freaked out about our move to Idaho, they really freaked out when I told them that I was now moving to South Carolina! Daniel was with us; Sarah and Jake were still in Idaho with their dad. I should never have left my children, even though they were with their father. I can see now how wrong it was, but at the time my decision-making skills were far from practical, reasonable, or in *anybody's* best interest.

Now we were in South Carolina; I was clear across the continent from my family, and I had no one except Daniel and Ray. I sank into a horrible depression and began to develop symptoms of bulimia *and* gained fifty pounds. I was binging and purging like crazy. All I did was sit in an apartment all day, watch TV, and eat. We lived in a predominantly African-American town, which was very hard on my son. He was jumped numerous times, had his bike and some other of his things stolen, and had other problems at school. Once again, Ray was not happy with his job and his health started to deteriorate even further because of his depression. He wanted to move again.

Believe it or not, we had tried many times to get married, all the way back from when we lived in Boise. It just never happened. Ironically, here, where we were the most miserable, we finally made it to the courthouse steps, and we got married.

ONCE

Marry me once;
I will be yours forever.

Hold my hand once;
I will never let go.

Look at me once;
My eyes will look to no other.

Carry me once;
I will feel safe forever.

Be sad just once;
I will comfort you always.

Hold me tight and don't let go, just once;
I will feel the warmth of your arms forever.

Make love to me once;
Our passion will last a lifetime.

Run your finger thru my hair once;
Forever will I feel its soothing touch.

Come home to me once;
Every day there I will be waiting.

Sing me a song once;
My ears will hear it always.

Make me laugh once;
It will bring a smile to my heart.

Cry on my shoulder once;
I will cry with you always.

Touch my face once;
The feeling will linger forever.

Fly with me once;
We will never come down.

Love me once;
I will love you forever.

AMEN

Climbing into bed, your scent surrounds me.
Its wraps me in its embrace.
It soothes and protect as it sets my heart free.

Never have I felt so protected in an embrace.
Hold me and never let me go.
Don't let me fall as you kiss my face.

My love for you is as powerful as the river flows.
It rises and falls,
It twists and turns, but its strength it grows.

The dance of life is one step at a time,
One foot in front of the other.
Our love is the music; it's the rhyme.

So much time we miss together each day.
It makes the day so long and sad.
But at the end of the day, I know it will be okay.

I listen to love songs and dream them of you.
They say in words what I cannot.
But I listen and love them and know they are true.

Words can be written with paper and pen,
But true love comes from the heart within.

But these words are from my heart,
I want you to know.
They are not words, they are art.

Because I speak them to the most precious of men,
The one I will love forever.
And that is a promise, Amen.

WILL YOU BE THERE?

When the shadows fall and the light changes,
Will you be there?
Sometimes in life, it rearranges.

When the distance we see starts closing in,
Will you be there?
For the other side is what we will win.

When hearts hurt and things are hard,
Will you be there?
What we have, is it enough to guard?

When my eyes are shut, and my lips closed tight,
Will you be there?
For what I am, am I enough for you to fight?

When the winds seem dead and tired,
Will you be there?
Is there still in me what you once admired?

When the sun rises in the morning,
Will you be there?
Or will it change and the rains begin pouring?

When our love is tested, as it will be,
Will you be there?
Or will it from me, you'll want to be free?

Will you be there when I laugh and cry?
Will you be there when I'm bold and shy?

Will you be there when I can't find my way?
Will you be there when I have a dark day?

Will you be there when I need your touch?
Will you be there because I love you so much?

Will you be there just to hold my hand?
Will you be there whether I fall or stand?

Will you be there for me to look upon your face?
Will you be there with me at the end of our race?

I think we were in South Carolina for maybe eight months. I even tried to get out of the house a little bit by getting a job at Lowes. It was supposed to be only part-time work, but it ended up being more of a full time job. My moods shot straight up to manic like a flash. I was taking overtime hours, not sleeping, and my mind was spinning out of control again. I felt so revved up that I couldn't stop! It was like pressing on the accelerator of a car and watching the RPMs go up, but no one was letting off of the acceleration or putting on the brake.

Because my stamina was so low, my breaking point was very short. I got sick and went to the doctor. While standing at the counter checking in, I fell to the floor and passed out cold. My job at Lowes was over; I had worked myself to exhaustion. I went to my psychiatrist and he tweaked my medications, which brought me back down again. I was reminded again that stress was not my friend. I rollercoastered from mania to depression quite frequently; this is called rapid-cycling. It can be hours, days, months, or years; at the time, mine seemed to be by the hour. This is why bipolar disorder is classified as a mood disorder. My moods were swinging all over the place by the hour or day. During the depression times, I was binging and purging terribly.

I can count three times in my life that I went through these episodes of binging and purging; all during very low, depression periods of my illness. The last time was when I was in South Carolina, and this was the only time I engaged in this behavior when I was actually having a problem with my weight. I had gotten to be about fifty pounds overweight, due mostly to medications and partly due to bad eating habits and no exercise. It was the first time in my life that I had gotten that heavy, and it only contributed to my depression.

I am so sensitive about my weight that I won't take any medication if weight gain is listed as a possible side effect. I guess my reasoning behind this is that I can either be fat and depressed or thin and manic! There must be a happy medium; right now I seemed to have found it, but it took quite a while. I just kept working at it until I found it. This can be particularly frustrating for the loved ones who live with or are involved with that person. The one with the bipolar is going to suffer, yes, because the highs and lows are very agitating and disrupting to your lifestyle, but excuses can be made. Those that have to deal with you on a regular basis, on the other hand, don't quite see it that way. It can drive them nuts trying to keep up, never knowing on a daily or even hourly basis what kind of mood or behavior they are going to be dealing with, and the drama … oh, the drama! Since someone with bipolar disorder on a manic swing is completely unpredictable, what they might say or do can draw drama like a magnet to steel. Consider, too, that loved ones also have to deal with the fallout of the addictions associated with the illness. There will almost always be some sort of addiction, and we all know that some can cause great harm and can even be life-threatening.

Ray got fired from his job. His depression was getting the best of him. He was missing a lot of work, and they got sick of it. He wanted to move to Washington. I did not. I couldn't do it again. My parents were really freaking out by now. They did not like Ray at all by this time, especially when seeing how badly my health was declining. They wanted me to come to the desert in California to live near them. Considering the situation I was in, I decided it was my only option. Ray decided to go to Washington without me; and the irony of it was this time we were actually married! Believe it or not, he left to go to Washington and left me and Daniel behind with my car and all our belongings in a storage unit. Daniel and I flew to California and *my parents* had to pay to have all of our things shipped out to California. We lived in my parents' guest room out of our suitcases for two months. My parents eventually bought us a house two miles from where they lived, put us in it, and said, "Sit, stay, and don't move!" That we did. Ray would fly out every month or so to see me. This arrangement lasted for only about six months. We eventually got a divorce. We were only actually married about seven or eight months, and of that time we were only together maybe two or three months. Even though things had gone so sour by this time, I still loved Ray very much, and it was a hard break up. We talked for quite some months after that, and Ray even moved to California to a hospital in Los Angeles, hoping that there might be a possibility of us reconciling in the future. We both knew down deep that this was very unlikely. We finally had to sever the ties completely and go our separate ways to be able to move on.

I sincerely hope that Ray finds the peace and happiness he is seeking in his life.

GOOD-BYE FOR NOW

Our time is gone; it's in the past.
How did we know it would not last?
It moved along way too fast.

Our love was deep, strong, and true,
But how could we know our days were few?

Our souls intertwined; yes, they did meet,
Like two lost lovers running through the street.
Intense it was; it created heat.

But time moves on without our choice.
It cares not; it has no voice.

Fate has written our names in the sand.
We do not know when it will use its hand.
Its hands, they are loose from its big bands.

Fate has chosen our paths, now we know.
Its choice it has made we don't want to show.
But in this life, we must go.

Nothing can take the love we did share,
And though it seems not, I do still care.
Thinking of my past without you, I do not dare.

A we together can no longer be said,
Though at one time our hearts were wed.

It's time to go to find our way.
Where we're at now we cannot stay,
Even though together you want to lay.

Our souls will forever know each other.
The love will be there that cannot be covered.

Take this time to remember me.
Open your eyes; you must see.
You know where life leads, what will be.

The seeds of my love for you will forever be sown.
I hope that that is what I have shown.
I want that to forever be known.

Good-bye for now, I will have to say.
But in my heart, you will forever stay.

CHAPTER 3
The Road Narrows

After my marriage to Ray ended, my life reached a significant turning point. I had fifty pounds to lose and my life to get back together again.

My parents bought me a house, so Daniel and I had a secure place to live; the first secure place I had again in almost two years. I found a mental health clinic where I was hooked up with a psychiatrist and a therapist that I saw on a regular basis; there I was able to begin again to try and get my illness to be manageable. I also went to regular group meetings once, and sometimes twice a week, for about a year. I began to swim and go to the gym regularly to get my body back into shape, along with adding a better diet. In about a year, I was back down to a normal weight. It seemed that things were looking up, as far as my security, needs, and cares were concerned. I had done what I could to get help with housing and welfare in order to help with my social security/disability, yet my income was still so small that we barely made ends meet each month. If not for the help and support of my family, we would never have been able to do it on our own.

I missed Ray terribly, and I had never been on my own in my adult life. I had married Gene when I was eighteen, and after divorcing him, I had gone to Lee and then to Ray; this was the first time I had found myself completely alone without a man in my life. It was not a good feeling to me. I felt like I had no identity of my own; I had always found my identity in the man that I was with, so this was new territory for me. I did some dating, but I found men severely lacking in what I was looking for. I felt like I was looking for a savior to come along and take away the burden of my sordid past; someone that wouldn't be threatened by it or look at me like I was a freak. This was not an easy task. I had to learn the right time to tell the person I was dating that I had bipolar disorder. Too soon would scare them for sure, but too late would seem like I might be trying to hide something; there is such a fine line.

I did date a man who actually broke up with me because of my bipolar; he said it scared him. He obviously was very uneducated about bipolar disorder, and I think that he just did not want to take the time to get to know me. People tend to judge based on stereotypes and preconceived ideas, not on what is truth. I admit I was very offended and had my feelings hurt, but I just decided that he was not worth the effort if that was his attitude. But hurt it did, all the same.

I believe all of us with a mental illness have experienced this at least once, probably more. There is a stigma attached to mental illness from a long history of it being looked at as a "madness" or "insanity." After all, what did they call institutions back in the day? They were insane asylums and mental institutions. You occasionally still hear people refer to them using those terms! And think about all the movies you see portraying psychiatric institutions. From *One Flew Over the Cuckoo's Nest* to *Girl, Interrupted* and *Shutter Island*; they just feed into that stigma all the more. If people don't have an understanding, they will just go by what they see and are told until they are educated with the truth.

The following poems describe the changes I was going through and my insecurities.

MY OWN PACE

My life has gone through so many changes,
And now again it rearranges.
Something new every time I turn the pages.

There is still something deep and cold inside of me.
A voice is there; it won't set me free.
No matter how I try, it won't let me be.
I cannot buy the peace that is in front of me.

The torture in my soul is there.
Does anyone of you even care?
This burden I have is too much to bear.

A love that is new, but heavy the price.
What will happen when I roll that dice?

My heart is torn; it aches inside.
Pain and hurt there does reside.
Everyone is against me; no one is on my side.

Everyone wants too much from me.
I need some space; just let me be.
I'm ready to break; can't you see?

I hide away in my safe place,
For nowhere else for me is there a space.
I've got to move at my own pace.

Don't tie me down to bind my hands.
Don't hold my soul, not in bands.

Love me strong and love me true.
Love away the ghosts; let them through.
Take my pain; make my soul new.

Take the old voices; chase them away.
Open the clouds; make it a new day.
Break through the hurt; make there a way.
I can't hold on; I'm slipping away.

The battle goes on inside my head.
Sometimes I can't even get out of bed.
I even forget the things I've said.

Confusion takes over every day.
My lips fumble and don't know what to say.
Sometimes I wonder if there ever will be a way.

Take my hand and pull me close.
Of your love, give me a dose.

Pull me from the hole I am in.
Show me how I can make it and win.
Wrap your arms around me and take away my sin.

SOMEDAY

A shadow passes across my face.
Where does it come from?
To me I don't know where is my place.

Lies are all that come from my mouth,
Though I try to make them stop.
I sit and I wonder, and I mourn in this house.

Blame me; it is my sin after all.
Thought not intended to hurt;
Sin that makes me take that fall.

Hurt I have caused in so many ways.
When will I be stopped?
All I see ahead are more and more days.

The train is moving; it won't slow its pace.
I'm on the tracks watching it come.
I feel like I am running with that train in a long race.

The shadow bears down on me growing darker.
The darkness scares me.
I look around I see it growing larger.

My soul is burning, burning to ash.
Why does it burn?
Why do I need to make that mad dash?

An explosion is near; it's at my front step.
It grows stronger and stronger.
It is a secret that only I have kept.

Just one last time is all I want.
What if I never get it?
To get it out so it will not haunt.

I want to go home where I belong.
I miss it so much.
Deep in my soul do I long.

Take me away from all that I cause,
The pain and the blame.
Just take me away, no need to pause.

What I'm looking for I'm not sure,
Peace and forgiveness?
But I do know this blame I must endure.

Someday I will know peace in my life.
I will set things right.
In my chest will no longer be that knife.

MY DREAMS

All my dreams, they have gone,
Like the light steps of a baby fawn.
Nothing gives me joy of the rising dawn.

What do I have in my life to be found?
I close my ears to block out the sound,
The sound of the nothingness that does abound.

I look around; no direction I see.
I wouldn't even know which way to flee.
Is this the life I wanted it to be?

There is no path for me to go.
Where are the seeds that I did sow?
I thought my life would just flow.

So many people I have hurt in my days.
The pain and the guilt of that just stays.
But get rid of it, people tell me; there are many ways.

Cutting seems the only way to take away the pain,
Like the drunk that falls down and cannot regain.
But it is only for a short time, and only in vain.

But how do I get relief from what is inside?
Who can take me off this crazy ride?
The river is grown now; it is so wide.

I see no future ahead of me.
There is nothing there for me to see.
Someone tell me just what will I be?

My past is weak; it has shown no mercy.
One day I was even told that I was crazy.

There are other lives that I hold in my hands.
Did I throw them to the winds to see where each lands?

My life is a lie.
I look around, and I wonder why.
Then I sit back and take a deep sigh.

The dreams that I will never see,
I look inside and the lie is me.
I will never be what I could be.

The tears are streaming down my face.
I want off; I no longer want to be in this race.
But I know I will never be where I want in my place.

What I want can never be replaced.
That has to realized, has to be faced.

Like an arrow shot crooked, my shot has missed.
I have been visited by an angel and have been kissed.

Facing my reality,
That is my destiny.
Making each day a new step, though it will be tiny.

Gene and I had gotten to be very close again. We talked quite a bit about reconciling. We knew, though, that at the time we were in two very different worlds, and it would never work for us then. Our children, believe it or not, did not want us to reconcile. They actually did not even like us to spend time together. When I would go to Idaho for a visit, Gene and I would go out together for dinner or out for drinks, and the kids would get mad at us. We had to make sure any time we spent together was always when the kids were around us. We knew that we still loved each other very much, but the timing for us was just not right. We had become two very different people than when we had been together. In the very deep talks that we had, we were able to resolve a lot of our past hurts, but it was understood that Gene would always have some trust issues with me because of the infidelity. I could accept this with complete understanding; I would not have expected anything less. I wrote these two poems to Gene.

A SPLIT IN TIME

I reach for you; you're there no more.
The love that remains reaches my very core.

In my heart there is still an ache.
Though I have to, I do; I don't want to fake.
I keep it inside for both our sakes.

A history we have; it was long and true,
Something that only a few can do.
Every day seemed something new.

A split in time, a moment of sin,
Took away what was within.

Two ways we went alone with fears;
No one there to dry our tears.
We could not listen blocked were our ears.

No one knew the pain we had.
The pain and hurt turned to sad.
Never could we know it could be so bad.

I think of you often in my dreams.
My past haunts me; I can hear my screams.

Maybe again someday our lives will cross;
Take the dice and make that toss.
The rock keeps rolling, gathering that moss.

In my heart, I hope someday
That for the two of us there will be a way
For us to live and together stay.

For now I know is not the time;
Who will know when that clock will chime.

Two different people, we have become.
But some of that happiness and peace, I want some.
Who knows, together to us it may come.

Don't forget me in that life of yours;
But be happy in what you do as your life soars.

MY DESTINY

My eyes are wet and my vision blurry,
For there is much that I have to worry.

You've been gone from my life so long ago,
But you are there, and the pain it is so.
Do I tear it from my heart to make it go?

A love that was to last forever,
Now we are on our own endeavor.
Time is cruel, sometimes its voice says never.

Why can't we control our own fate?
We can only close our eyes and just wait.
Who is going to be there to open that gate?

I am lost at the hands of destiny.
So much emptiness there is found in me.

One day my world just slipped away,
Never to return; it would not stay.
There was nothing that I could even say.

Now I look, and I want it back.
But to turn around time, it is like an attack.
I'm a woman in mourning; I'm dressed in black.

The future I see is my own headstone.
There is no one around; it is all alone.
The wind in the trees sounds like a moan.

Come to me there, the love I have lost.
Hurry with haste, no matter the cost.

Put your headstone beside me; together we'll be.
To the sky we will look; we both can see.
In heaven together we will walk; this will be our destiny.

I learned around the middle of 2007 that I was going to be a grandmother. This was shocking news to me. Sarah was only nineteen years old; she was not in a relationship and this pregnancy was not exactly planned. She was very upset that she was pregnant; her fear and anxiety was overwhelming. I was worried that she might not carry the baby, but it was too late to do anything about it. For this I was very thankful, and of course, now I am very grateful to have my "little man," as I call my grandson Shayde. As all of us mothers have in all of the centuries before us, she overcame her fear and trepidation and did just fine. She is a wonderful mother to my beautiful grandson, and he has a very loving, attentive daddy who takes very good care of him.

I wrote this poem for Sarah when she was struggling with becoming a new mother.

EACH MOMENT

In you new life grows,
A part of your soul still unknown,
Some of those seeds that you have sown.

Each kick inside reminds you he's there.
He's depending on you, needing your care.
But you look in your heart and wonder where.

Never will we know where our lives will be.
If only we could look ahead and just see.
Sometimes we turn that corner and wonder "why me?"

Your line is drawn; your course is set.
There is no more time to place that bet;
No time to look back with regret.

Soon you will know the helplessness of a child.
Your days are gone of being wild.

You will hear the very first breath your child will take.
The depths of your soul will be touched make no mistake.
His tiny fingers will hold yours and make your heart ache.

A mother's love is not learned.
A mother's love is not earned.
In your heart your love is burned.

The aches and pains of now will go away.
But forever a mother you will always stay.
The feeling in your stomach means it starts today.

Enjoy each moment now for it won't last forever.
Let your memories be good of you and your baby together.
Be patient, gentle, and calm as a floating feather.

I remember wrapping my arms around my daughter inside
me.
When she arrived, I held her as close as could be.
You will know; you will see.

She is a woman now, and she is bringing a gift to me.
My love for her is stronger than it could be.
She was a blessing then, and a blessing now to me.

I had been walking for exercise when I was not swimming. I had a route through the neighborhood that was a two-mile walk. I walked by this one particular house where I ran into its occupant on occasion. His name was Norm. We chitchatted now and then, until one day we talked, and he invited me in to see his house that he had been fixing up. He had lived in that house for twenty years and had just gutted it out and redone it completely. He was a very nice man, and he invited me out to dinner; thus began a new relationship for me.

Norm was a very amazing person. Very gentle, kind, loving, and he would do absolutely anything for me. He loved me very, very much. I could not have asked for more. We were together for about a year and a half.

Unfortunately, Norm had me at a difficult time. I was going through some new things that I didn't quite understand. I was beginning to have flashbacks. The flashbacks were from past traumas; Lee's death, carrying immense guilt over my children, a lot of sexual issues in regards to my sexual abuse and being molested that I wasn't even quite aware of yet were all lying under the surface waiting to emerge. Norm was handling things as best as he could, but the hard part was that my cutting was getting to be out of control again, and this time it was becoming alarmingly life threatening.

The psychiatrist I had been seeing had left, and I had gone through a couple of doctor changes, which is an extremely difficult thing for me to do. I don't handle change very well, and breaking in a new doctor who doesn't know anything about me and my past is very, very frustrating for me. It seems like they always want to change my medications. Every doctor seems to have a *better* way; well, I don't think they do, and I usually tell them so. I can be a very difficult patient at times like this, but I feel I am protecting myself. It has taken me so long to find the right combination of medications. I don't like another doctor coming in and trying to change things when they don't even know anything about me yet. This attitude of mine, though, has gotten me into many nasty exchanges with more than one doctor in my past; yet, I have won each time. I call it "advocating for myself." It has to be done. We know ourselves best; we have to be in tune to our bodies and know what works best for *us*. Fortunately, I was eventually assigned a new doctor who knew what he was doing and was able to work with me.

The therapist I was with was very distressed by my cutting, as was my doctor. By the end of 2007, I was cutting terribly and often. My cuts were deeper and causing more damage. I had even severed a nerve in my leg that cut off all feeling to the top of my leg right over my knee cap. I am still waiting for the rest of the feeling to come back to that area. It seemed like the only thing anyone could do was just keep giving me more and more drugs. It was beginning to become a vicious cycle and going nowhere. My time was running out. This is what I wrote about the drugs.

BEDSIDE TABLE

Pile of pills on the bedside table.
The only thing that makes me able.
Able to live in a world that has given me a label.

Today the sadness closes in on my heart,
Sometimes things feel normal, I forget that they aren't.

Under the surface there's a current that flows.
Unseen from above, the depths of pain still grows.
No one can tell, they would never know.

Nothing ever really takes it away.
Things from the past still haunt as much today.
Never is it black or white, it's always grey.

The soft light of the room takes me back,
Like the shadows of my mind some light thru the crack.

The driving beat of the music hides in the shadows of the light.
Will my demons ever go away and make this right?
Forever will I have to fight?

Love me strong, make me your mine.
Draw a circle around me, make it a red line.
Hurt me no more, make everything fine.

My tears are falling, they drop to the floor.

Will you turn and run for the door?
My pain burns to my very core.

I know what I am and will always be,
In my past I will forever see.

My scars remind me of all that I have lost.
But I will never know what the cost.
There is so much that I have lost.

Give me something to make me stable,
Reach again for the bedside table.

On December 22, I got a call from my daughter that she was going into labor. Shayde was not due until early January, and I had a flight scheduled for then. I was absolutely devastated that I was not going to be there when my grandson was born. I cried all day. All I could think about was the fact that my family was scattered about because of me, and that if it wasn't for me, we would all be together. I would be away from my daughter when she needed me the most. It was a crushing blow to me. I cannot even express to you how morbidly distraught I was that I could not be by my daughters side at this crucial time; I was insane with grief. Interestingly, on this day that my grandson was about to be born was also my daughter's twentieth birthday. I got up to Idaho as fast as I could.

There was a lot of snow. I will never forget that about the trip. I happen to love snow, and it seems that a lot of my memories are linked to what the weather was like during particular events. That visit proved to be one of the most memorable ones and the most difficult ones I have ever had.

I will never forget the first sight of my grandson; he was a true miracle to me. I wrote this poem about him when he turned one week old. I was still reeling from the fact that I was a grandmother to this small treasure.

ONLY ONE WEEK

Soft breath through tiny lips;
Tiny fingers touch my finger tips.

Your eyes search then lock on mine.
You scrunch your face with a whimper and a whine.

My heart softens as I look at your face.
There is no other that could take your place.

A tear slips slowly down my cheek.
Today you have turned only one week.

The palm of my hand cradles your head.
I lie with you quietly across the bed.
There are no words, none to be said.

Your tiny hand grasps my finger.
I only want to stay and linger.

Kissing you softly upon your brow,
You are so perfect; I don't know how.
All I know is you are here right now.

I don't want to leave you; I love you so.

I want to stay and watch you grow.

But always know I am only steps away.
My heart beats for you in every way.

A part of me you will always be.
No one can take that; it's for all to see.
My grandson, forever, so special to me.

I've told you a little bit about how precarious my relationship
with Jake, my oldest son, is. The only time he really
communicates with me is when I am actually in Idaho.
That is the only time he actually acknowledges me, more or
less; but when I am there, we get along great, and I have a
good time with him. I have also told you how my kids don't
like Gene and me spending time alone together. Well, one
night Gene and I decided to go out to the local bar (there is
only one; this is a rinky-dink town of eight hundred outside
of Boise) for a drink and to play some pool. It was literally
barely half a mile down the street. Gene had gotten a little
tipsy, and we were laughing and having fun as we walked
in the cold, snowing night air to the car. Gene grabbed me,
spun me around, and kissed me. No big deal; just a fun
smack on the lips, no making out or anything.

Now, you have to understand how a small town works
if you have never lived in one. There is one basic rule: if you
don't want anyone to know your business, move to a bigger
town. In this town, you don't get away with anything. In
fact, Sarah and I look so much alike that I am mistaken
for her constantly while I am in town. So, needless to say,
someone in the parking lot saw that kiss, and by the time

we got the half mile back home, all hell had broken loose. Sarah was in the bedroom crying, and Jake was fuming and ready to take on his dad. I chose to handle Sarah. The story had come through from a friend of Sarah's that we had been making out in the parking lot of the bar (of course).

Things began to suddenly spiral way out of control. Sarah believed the *true* story, but was mad that it now was creating a rumor. Jake on the other hand was livid. He did not like the fact that we had been together at all; although he had no idea as to why this bothered him so much. There was a lot of yelling, and Jake left. Things right in here get a bit fuzzy for me, but I know that Jake came back because his dog was still there, and I was hoping that he had calmed down enough for me to talk to him. I didn't know exactly what I was going to say, but I wanted him to know the truth. I also wanted him to understand that his dad and I were adults, and so was he. He needed to let us live our own lives as we chose, and we really didn't need to be accountable to him for what we did, especially when we hadn't done anything wrong. We wanted him to know we respected his discomfort about us being together, and we acted accordingly most of the time, this situation just happened to get out of control.

When Jake walked back into the house, he was anything but calm. I approached him to try to talk, but he was having nothing of it. Jake is a very mellow, low-key kind of kid. It takes a lot to get him riled. But when he blows, he blows hard and long. He began to leave, and I made the mistake of trying to get in his way to stop him; he pushed me out of the way. As he pushed me, he called me the most horrible names I could ever be called by anyone, least of all my own son. I was devastated. I couldn't believe my ears. Now I became angry from the hurt. Gene was out in the car waiting for Jake. I chased after him. They were pulling out the drive starting down the street. I ran after the car banging on the passenger side. Gene slowed the car, and I swung open the passenger door where Jake was. I started yelling at him that he had no right to call me those things and to be angry at me, that I had done nothing wrong. He spit on me and kept calling me horrible names. Gene yelled at me to get back and he drove off. I slumped to my knees in the muddy, snowy gravel and cried like I have never cried before. I felt like my guts had just been ripped from my body. My heart was truly broken. I got up and started walking, just walking. I didn't even have a jacket, and it was below freezing. I was crying hysterically; I'm surprised no one saw me, but it was very late at night.

I found a deserted lot down the street where there were just some old junked-out cars. I paced around and I screamed at God. I was angry at him for all the things he had taken from me. My family was in ruins; we had lost everything and it was all because of what had happened to me. I was so angry at God for that. I took on everything that happened to all of us and put it on me. I was the one who always held us all together, and now look at us; we were here because of me.

I had lost Jake for good. I had never felt so much despair. I couldn't understand why all this had happened to me. I just wanted to die. It was the first time that I had actually felt so completely hopeless that I felt like giving up. I became exhausted and spent from my grief. Not a tear was left in me; I lay down in the snow and decided I was just going to go to sleep. I figured if I went to sleep I would just freeze to death in my sleep, and I would never even know it. I laid there and thought that there wasn't anyone who really needed me anyway. Even my new grandson; he would just never know me, so it would make no difference to him. My other son was always mad at me, too. Sarah and my parents were the only ones that I knew would really miss me, and my sister. I convinced myself that they would soon get over it.

So, I fell asleep. So at peace, it felt good. I completely accepted my choice and felt an overwhelming calmness take over. Then a car drove by. They didn't see me; I was lying in the snow behind an old car. But I knew they were looking for me. It woke me up; I was mad. Damn it! I just wanted to die! Can't they just leave me alone! Then I thought of Sarah and little Shayde again. I had to get up. And even Daniel, though he was mad at me 99 percent of the time, I guess he still needed me. I began to walk back to the house. I was wet and caked with snow. Gene drove up and found me about a block away from the house.

That was a very long night, and from it came these two poems.

LET THE COLD TAKE MY SOUL

Shards of glass inside make me bleed.
Harsh voices smother me; I cannot breath.

I'm lying in the snow; just let me sleep.
My eyes are blurry; I can only weep.
Secrets remain I cannot keep.

Spit on my face, harsh words to my ear.
From my own body came the person that the voice I now hear.
I am so far away, but the cold is so near.

Take me now; let the cold take my soul.
There is nothing left, only a hole.

I am so tired; I just want to sleep.
Forever to sleep, let it be deep.
The cold envelopes me as I lie here and weep.

My body is throbbing with pain and wailing.
Where do I go from here, there is no telling.

I can take no more; my strength has given out.
Why is this happening again? What is it all about?

I can hardly take another breath.
All I want is to see my own death.

There is no fight left in me.
I look ahead; there is nothing to see.
I have lost so much; what next will there be?

It will never stop, the sins of my past.
No matter how long, it is back in a flash.
Everything I try to rebuild has turned to ash.

It will never stop, this pain in my heart.
My life will always be torn apart.
My own blood will spill, never to make a new start.

THREE HEARTS

Three hearts that beat in tune with mine,
Their blood is from me.
I was their lifeline.

Scratches and spit across my face,
Ugly words that cut to my core.
I don't know anymore where is my place.

From my soul love still abounds.
It is bottomless.
Look and see; there is no end to be found.

The body that gave life has been torn apart.
So much pain, my knees are on the ground.
There is no beginning; where is the start?

Insides are burning; tears fall like rain.
Children's faces are no longer there.
Growing and hurting, what is there to gain?

Did I do this?
Torture three souls?
Am I a murderess?

Am I to pay for the sins of three?
Because I brought life,
The sins of three plus me?

My heart does not ache; it is ripped in two.
I carry it and carry it every day.
It never goes away; can you see it when I look at you?

Don't they know?
For them I give all,
Of this I only show.

I can still feel the kick of their tiny feet,
The agony as their body tore from mine,
The light in their eyes when the world it was time to meet.

Now that light has turned dark on me.
My arms are still open.
And though pain I feel, a mother I will always be.

I endured the rest of the trip by just focusing on my little grandson and my daughter. It was a very hard time for me, though. Of course, I didn't talk to Jake for a couple of days. Before I left we were talking again, but nothing was resolved. I tried desperately to get him to talk to me once I was home again. I sent text messages and left voice messages like crazy, but he never responded to them. Here is a poem I wrote to him after I had been home for about six weeks.

MEMORIES WILL FADE

I see your face in the picture by my bed.
There are so many things that need to be said.

You are the one so special to me.
Just look in my eyes; can't you see?
What is it that you want me to be?

The love I have for you can't be taken away.
But you are silent; you have nothing to say.
The light in your eyes has turned gray.

Every day you take a piece of my heart.
Don't you see you are tearing me apart?
I thought we could stop, make a new start.

Open your soul, look inside.
Open your heart, open it wide.
What do you see? What does reside?

Inside there is a man trying to escape the boy,
But to get to the man you must destroy the boy.
Maybe then in your life you can find some joy.

You are stronger than you think you are.
Your journey in life will take you far.

Share with me the journey you're on.
I love you and want to share your song.
A mother's love can never go wrong.

The little boy that wanted to ease his mother's day,
He is still there, how I want him to stay.
But the man he wants to be you cannot betray.

Please forgive me for the hurt I have caused you.
All that matters now is the love I have for you is true.
Memories will fade, and soon there will only be few.

The love I have for you will never be lost.
It always stayed, no matter the cost.
I had many bridges that had to be crossed.

But now I am here for you, never to go away.
I promise you now, no matter what, I will always stay.

Perhaps one day I will write a sequel to the following poem. I have always had a strong belief and faith in God. However, like many, my faith had been tested, and I was questioning whether God was really looking out for my best interest. Yes, I became angry at Him. Those feelings are long gone, and I still don't have the answers as to why God let me go through the things that I have, but I have come to realize that I don't have to have all the answers right now. I just need to go on and try to help others through my own experiences, and being angry at Him will certainly not accomplish anything.

DEAR GOD

Look at me now; I am afraid of you.
And to you who I thought I would always be true.

I look to the sky, and the color is gray.
I wonder why; I don't even want to pray.

I did everything you asked me to,
But you took my life away, didn't you?
I want to understand, but your answers are few.

Is it punishment of me that you seek?
Why? Because I have been weak?

Did you give me my family just to take it away?
Look at my life; it has turned to decay.

This madness I have, did you give it to me?
What is in my future that you can see?
Where is it that I will be?
Will you continue to take from me?

My faith in you used to be strong.
Now I don't know where I belong.
Is it me? Am I so wrong?

I don't feel you anymore; you are so far away.
Is it there that you are going to stay,
Now that you have left me this way?

Whatever happened to "Footsteps in the Sand"?
I thought you would at least hold my hand.

I know that you are there,
But for me, do you really care?

So sad, all I can do is cry.
You're not there who wipe the tear from my eye.
To me did you say good-bye?

Norm and I broke up at some point around here. I was feeling a little closed in, and I needed some space from him. I also was having some harsh flashbacks; regarding Lee, but also the rapes that I had endured. I was feeling really confused about a lot of things in my life. I was attending school at the community college near my house. I had been going for about a year at this point, and although I loved it, it was very stressful, especially math; it was particularly difficult for me and still is. Even being on the Dean's list, I am still on my third semester of algebra. I attribute my struggle partly to my medications that largely affect my memory and concentration.

I had been meeting lots of new people, young people; particularly younger men. I began seeing some of them. I went through this very strange period of dating men much younger than me. I also started frequenting the bars and clubs again. For a time, I lived a sort of double life. There was the daytime Tina who was a single mom who went to college, and then there was the night life Tina. She was quite the opposite, and I found myself getting into trouble again. Behavior similar to previously, yet not quite as bad. My poetry also got dark (darker than usual), and I was cutting severely.

Something was going on in me, yet I couldn't put my finger on just exactly what it was. I felt very scared and out of control. Since it was just Daniel and me, of course he took on the role of the man of the house. Like his brother, he too had always been very protective of me. It disturbed him seeing the young men that I was dating; so much so, that he threw a little fit one night and kicked in the side door of the car of someone that I had been seeing. Although I tried to be the authority figure in the house, because I had lost that status so many years ago, I could never get it back. Daniel and I did manage to have a pretty good relationship, though, considering my failing health once again. Of course, because I knew I couldn't control him as a parent, I pretty much let him do what he wanted, putting down *some* boundaries, such as a mutual respect and consideration of each other. He managed to stay within those limits, for a while anyway. Yet, at this particular time, I was in an agonizing battle with my head, but I couldn't put my finger on what it was, so my symptoms became out of control again.

I WILL CROSS EACH LINE

Don't turn around; it's already gone.
There are so many things that were so wrong
Open your ears; listen to that song.
I feel you still, though you've been gone so long.

Where are you? As I look to the sky,
Still I sit and wonder why.
The thoughts of you still make me cry.

I've lost so much along the way.
My mouth opens, but what can I say?
God has forgotten me; I won't even sit and pray.

I thought the pain would grow less with the time,
But the knife in my heart only turns as the clock does
chime.

My eyes grow wild with this fever.
How long am I going to be a griever?
I won't listen to your words anymore; I am not your
believer.

You take and never give back;
Parts of my life will forever be black.
The blood in my veins seeps through that crack.

Don't look at me that way; I know what you think.
It was poison that you gave me to drink.
Now where I stand is beginning to sink.

What would have been different in another life?
Would there have been so much strife?
Would I have turned to that knife?

Looking down at me, what do you see?
Do you see the woman that I could be?
Or is there no such thing, only a maybe?

Can I be unburied from this grave where I rest?
The headstone lies heavy upon my chest.
Don't lie to me; it's not real, it's only a test.

I will finish this life of mine.
I will follow each sign.
Through each twist and turn, I will cross each line.
That road is narrow; each line is so fine.

SET ME FREE

The sky is heavy, it's pressing down on me.
The clouds cover my eyes; I cannot see.
Where do I go? What do I want to be?

I look around this place; I am all alone.
A noise comes from my chest; it is a groan.
Where will this path lead me? Where will I roam?

This life has taken me so many places.
I have looked upon so many faces,
Never to depend upon their good graces.

Take this life from me; it is worthless.
With so much pain, what is the difference?

Alone I am; there is no one near me.
Look in my eyes; you can only agree.
Cut out my heart; set me free.

When will it be my time to settle the score?
Will the lock forever be on that door?
Pain and heartache is mine forevermore.

Count the scars upon my body;
Each one there tells a story,
But in none of them is any glory.

Again will that blade be in my hand?
In my head will it always take its stand?
Across my arm its touch will land.

Sorry I am not; the pain needs release.
It's the only way to get some peace.

Someday I may find a better way,
But all I know now is that it is not today.
Today my sky it looks so gray.

The music is playing in my ears.
The softness of the sound matches my tears;
On it plays, calming my fears.

Tomorrow I will look for better days.
I will try as I can with all my ways.

TURNING TO GRAY

I'm drowning in my sorrow.
I cannot wake and deal with tomorrow.

I want to cut; the blade is calling me.
I need to see the blood to set me free.
These thoughts in my head won't let me be.

The confusion in my head won't let me rest.
I try so hard to be strong; I do my best.

Everyone expects so much from me.
The burden I'm under, why can't they see?
I'm trying to breathe; get away from me.

I close my eyes, but the screams I still hear.
I want to run, but I can't go anywhere.
People don't know; they just look and stare.

I am trapped in this room; I want to fly.
But instead, I pull my hair and cry.
Sometimes it would be easier to just say good-bye.

I don't want to feel; I want to be numb.
I want peace; how do I get some?

I don't want to remember anything.
Memories just hurt; they bite and they sting.
Take them all away on the bird's wing.

Just close my eyes; let me sleep.
I cannot stop; my eyes, they will still weep.
The pain in me, it goes so deep.

Open me up; take it all away.
Don't try to talk; there is nothing you can say.
The shadows they are coming; it's all turning to gray.

My cutting became so severe that on two separate times it took twenty-five staples to put my leg back together after a brutal cutting episode. It was like a drug addict who had to keep using more and more drugs to get the high. I needed to cut more and deeper. I would slice over and over on the same spot until I felt the release I was seeking, but the damage I was leaving looked like a horror movie. How could I do this, you ask? You go into a state of dissociation. This is a simple dictionary definition of dissociation.

Dissociation is a person's unconscious attempt at self-protection against an overwhelming and traumatic experience, such as may result from severe and prolonged maltreatment, sexual abuse, and/or neglect during childhood. The mind separates itself from an event or the environment so it can maintain some degree of order and sense.

Dissociation responses vary by individual. However, some common dissociation experiences include:

- Feelings of "standing outside" oneself or "watching from a distance" during a traumatic event.
- Developing significant personality changes and problems with mental processes.
- Incomplete or lack of memory of traumatic events.

- Appearing to have no sense of emotion regarding traumatic events.
- Dissociation that does not resolve on its own or is causing behavior or mental health problems requires professional counseling. Medications may also be used as part of treatment.

Dissociation is a coping skill (an unhealthy one), that I had developed over my lifetime to deal with many different issues. It was something that I had to learn to stop doing in order to stop cutting.

I literally had to hold my leg together as I drove myself to the hospital to get the gaping hole in my leg put back together. The looks of shock and revulsion on the nurses' and doctors' faces sobered me to what I had done. It was getting way out of control, and I couldn't stop it. I didn't know what was wrong with me! I was still seeing my doctors, even though my therapist had given up on me; she had turned me over to other therapists in the clinic who knew more about this particular addiction. Now they too were desperate for a solution that no one seemed to have. The state hospital was looming before me like a death sentence, because death was surely what was to be my prognosis.

Then one day one of my therapists found a hospital in Torrance, California, which specialized in trauma recovery; dealing with cutting was one of their specialties. There could be hope for me yet. We made a phone call to see if they could get me in. After a twenty minute conversation with the director of the hospital, I learned that I would be checking in within the next forty-eight hours. This would finally prove to be my salvation. This is where I was at mentally just before I went into the hospital.

TO DIE IS WELCOME

Where is death? I want to meet him.
There is this big empty hole in which I swim.
The noose is hanging from the broken limb.

My chest is empty; where is my heart?
I remember now, it fell apart.
There is no way to make a new start.

Don't look in my eyes; all you will see is a broken soul.
It's too late; I have lost all control.

The sky is falling like shards of glass.
The blood runs red through the green grass.
No shards remain; all must pass.

To die is welcome to take away the pain.
Just close my eyes; there is much to gain.
Death is coming like the falling rain.

All I have done, there is no forgiveness.
Take my word; there is no witness.
The seeds I have sown will only grow ugliness.

The whore has watched the sun come up.
The blood that runs could fill a cup.
What is inside is ready to erupt.

There is no freedom from the pain and the shame.
What you have to offer? It's all the same.
Death is simple; there is no game.

What would it take to end my life?
To take away the pain and the strife?
I know what to do with the blade of a knife.

What is it that my headstone would say?
Beloved mother that did betray?
Here is the whore; here is where she lay.

Death is the only way to stop my madness.
To those around me, it is only fairness.

CHAPTER 4
Yield to Oncoming Traffic

My mom and my sister drove me the two and a half hours to where I would reside for the next month. I showed up to Del Amo Hospital packed and ready for my stay, quite leery and wary of what was going to take place here. I had many memories of past hospital stays swimming through my head, none of them very pleasant.

I already knew from my experiences that I was going to be stripped of all the things that were comforts to me: my own pillows, blankets, my stuffed dog that I slept with every night, and even most of my favorite clothes and jewelry, because it was not allowed for various reasons. There was nothing allowed that had any kind of string or belt; therefore, sweatshirts and such had to have drawstrings pulled out of them. I could not have any blow dryer or curling irons because they had cords on them, and I could not have any make-up compacts with mirrors in them. I also had to keep all shampoos and cosmetics at the nurses' station and only used them when I took a shower in the mornings. I could not have an iPod or any source of music whatsoever.

We were kept on a hospital-type wing with three to a room, and the bathroom was one large room that we all shared; it was a hike down the hall past the nurses' station. There were only three showers to about twelve of us, so we had to get up early (around five or six in the morning) to get a shower. There was no privacy at all; if you had to go "number two," you would run the sink water to help drown out any noise. That was the most privacy you had in the bathroom. We got to know each other really quick and really well!

Our schedule was ruthless. We started sessions at 7:30 AM and went until 4:30 PM every day except weekends. We were in a lockdown facility, so we had to go through three locked doors to get to the cafeteria three times a day for meals. You didn't get a choice if you wanted to go or not; you went whether you ate or you didn't eat. The nurses kept watch on you 24/7. They logged what you were doing every moment of every day. We saw our therapist three times a week and our doctors every day. We did medications every morning and every night, and we took vitals every morning at 6:30 AM and every night at 9:00 PM. None of this was negotiable; if you didn't comply, they simply kicked you out. It was not like being in a regular psychiatric hospital; this was voluntary. You agreed to accept all these restrictions and regulations. That was the point; you were there to seek help, and that is what you got if you did it their way.

Visiting hours were only three hours a day on the weekdays and a bit longer on the weekends. I didn't have many visits because my family was a bit of a distance, but my sister came a couple times a week and always brought me some goodies: food, pictures, things that my nephews would make for me, and some crafty-type projects to work on in my spare time. My parents came a couple of times, but it was hard on them, especially my dad, to see me there. It was especially hard when they left and the door was locked behind them as they walked away.

So what exactly did they do for me? The first thing they did was open me up and completely break me apart. In our group sessions, they taught me how to express anger at those that had hurt me in my past; that is where I began.

Once the anger came out and I directed it where it was supposed to go instead of at myself, the ball began to roll. They continued to tear me all apart and work through the things I had endured, and then they began to put me back together again. It's called cognitive-behavioral therapy. It's all about confronting your fears and issues and dealing with them, not running and hiding from them or covering them up. Bit by bit, they built me back up and taught me coping skills to use when faced with things that were emotionally difficult for me to handle. It takes twenty-one days to make or break a habit; we practiced these skills of how to recognize what was going on inside of us physically, emotionally, and spiritually, and we learned how to keep ourselves grounded continuously throughout each day. Soon this becomes part of your routine every day, a habit. You become so in tune with yourself that eventually it begins to make it easier to deal with daily situations and stress. This is also where I learned how to stop using dissociation. That, I think, was one of the most difficult things to implement into my wellness program. I was so conditioned to using it, that I didn't even realize when I was doing it. I do still struggle with it some, but I am more likely to catch it and stop myself than I was before.

The therapist I had was very good. She was very compassionate, yet firm and strong without being leading or misguiding. I came to learn some things about my past that I had not yet brought to the surface with her help. I stress, though, that she was not leading in any way. It came to the surface that I had been molested by an older man when I was a child. It was a strange revelation because I felt like I always knew it, like it really wasn't a surprise; I had just finally acknowledged it. At first I was very calm. I told her what I had learned, and she asked me why I thought that, and I began telling her all these reasons. Things were just popping into my head like crazy; all the things that finally made sense. It just seemed so obvious; how could it have taken me so long to have figured this out? She said that she suspected this had been an issue for me, but she was waiting for me to discover it on my own. I left her office peacefully, yet the storm was brewing.

Later that afternoon, I suddenly felt like someone was squeezing my throat. My heart started pounding; I was having a panic attack. I started having flashbacks, not of actually being molested because I was too young when it happened, but all the scenarios around it and anger at the person who did it. I was getting incredibly anxious and scared. I told a nurse what was going on, and she called the director and my therapist. They came quickly and it wasn't drugs that they gave me; they took me out into the yard alone. I was crying by now and very upset. They said to just walk and talk; yell, scream, and cry, whatever I had to do to get it all out. So that is what I did. I kept going till I was exhausted. I cried, I yelled, I cursed, I screamed, and I walked and I walked. They just talked me through it. It took a while, but when I was done, I went in and lay down and I felt completely depleted. I felt like I had come to terms with it finally. Of course we addressed it some more in therapy and in sessions, but it was what they taught me about how to cope with my emotions when they rise up in front of me that was the most important thing. This was what I was here for. And this is what I left with.

I went into Del Amo Hospital in July of 2008; I have not cut since then. It was a life-altering experience for me, one I will never forget and one that probably saved my life.

I wrote this poem in the hospital.

STRENGTH CAN BE MINE

What am I on my own?
What is it that my life has shown?

Why can't I just be?
I look in the mirror, and what do I see?

A shell of a woman whose life has been taken away.
What does it mean to look forward to new day?

I crumble up and hide inside myself even more.
Which direction do I go? Which is the right door?
Does it show on my face? Can you see that I am a whore?

Take me away from the life that I lead.
All I feel is the need to bleed.
The desire to see red is like hunger or greed.

You shudder with fear at the words that I say,
Maybe I can make you understand someday.
Show you the fear of my own, that you might see, I pray.

My soul is dark from the mask of my sin.
I wait for the day that I will be new again.

Unzip my skin and set my heart free.
Is there such a thing as a happy me?
Or carrying this burden, will I always be?

I want to fill the emptiness in my soul.
Am I destined to always have this hole?
Changing this destiny must be my goal.

Those who have taken away my life,
I will take back and end this strife.
I will unlodge and remove from my back that knife.

Strength can be mine if I want to win.
Forever doesn't have to be the word tied to my sin.

In the following poems, I either don't remember exactly what was going on when I wrote them, or there just isn't much to say about them. But they all have a great expression of emotion in them that make them important to include. Having a mood disorder is very difficult to live with, as well as exhausting. As my bipolar is classified as being rapid cycling, some days my head could feel like a yo-yo, as my moods bounced up and down and everywhere in between. Sometimes poems just begin in my brain, and once the floodgate opens, words begin to pour out of me. It doesn't always have to be a major incident going on in my life to provoke a poem from me. I'll leave it to your imagination to guess my moods as I wrote these poems.

DO WITH IT AS YOU MUST

Through the mist I see your face.
The wind blows my dress that falls like lace.

Hold my hand; never let go.
Do you know that I need you so?

Touch my cheek; catch my tear.
With you beside me, there is no fear.

Your lips they whisper; they say my name.
Each touch of your hands, I feel no shame.
For I know you love me; there is no blame.

Never let go as the years go by.
Give no reason to make me cry.

From the beginning of time, I have been yours.
Between you and I, there are no closed doors.

My heart is yours until the end.
Although we don't know what is around the next bend.

Even in death, I'll be by your side.
An eternity is how long I'll be on this ride,
Because with you I have nothing to hide.

My soul is yours; I've given it to you.
Do with it as you must do.

PIECES OF MY HEART

Broken and gathered are the pieces of my heart.
Never could I think of making a new start.

Hide those pieces from the world outside.
There is no other in which to confide.
So many days of tears I have cried.

There is a wall that cannot be broken;
Pain unknown, not ever to be spoken.

If you look past the shadow you will see fear.
I turn my eyes so I will not shed that tear.

Cold and alone, will I forever be?
The world is dark and cruel; that is all I can see.

A hand brushes through the back of my hair.
I turn and look and can only stare.

The eyes are soft, dark, and deep.
The gentleness there makes me want to weep.

An arm pulls me close to a strong embrace.
I can only look up to an unimagined face.

The safety I feel makes the fear slip away.
I close my eyes … here is where I want to stay.
Suddenly things look not so gray.

Soft kisses and words across my cheek,
My heart begins to soften though words I cannot speak.
As the wall begins to crumble, my legs grow weak.

Strong arms lift me gently and carry me.
My arms go around his neck hopefully.
Is this what it feels like to finally be free?

The love I am feeling melts the pieces of my heart.
For now I know, I am ready to make a new start.

IF TOMORROW I WAS GONE

If tomorrow I was gone, would you be sad?
Or that my suffering was over, would you be glad?

You would no longer feel the softness of my kiss.
The whispering of my love in your ear, would you miss?

The feel of my touch on your skin would turn cold.
What about the talks of our lives as we grow old?

The smile on my face is only a memory to you now,
But the vision fades as you reach for it, somehow.

See my hair spread out across the pillow as you love me.
Did you ever think that this is how it would be?

All the talks we had so late into the night.
I tried … I did, with all my might.
But I lost … I lost the fight.

Now your arms are empty; will you cry?
But one thing is true: my love you can't deny.

Now you are standing on the cold ground.
My headstone is solemn; it makes no sound.

Feel my spirit as I touch your cheek.
You know I am there, though words I cannot speak.

From my pain and shame I am now free.
Your angel now is what I will be.
In the darkness of night, reach out; you might touch me.

CONFUSION

Who out there can really know me?
Stand back … don't get close enough to see me.
My heart is closed; I won't let you in.
This battle, I promise, you will not win.
This is just the way it must be.

I hold my soul; it is mine alone.
Watch yourself … I can't take that tone.
Don't you know it will make me cry?
You don't have to ask the reason why.
The pain inside comes out as a soft moan.

You can leave; it's happened before.
I know how to even the score.
Close up inside … block out the pain.
There is nothing here in which to gain.
Just turn around and shut that door.

I don't really want life now.
It's too hard … I don't know how.
It's all the same … bullshit on a plate.
Ultimately, we all have the same fate.
How far we go is what we allow.

We see new life in our children's eyes.
They look back and see only lies.
Is that what I've taught with this life of mine?
I know it is, but I won't whine.
Just close my ears; don't listen to their cries.

Confusion is all that's in my head today.
I look in all directions but can't find the way.

I'm holding on tight but losing my grip.
The pain on my back is from the lash of that whip.
Misery is here, so why do I stay?

The pit that I'm in has sunken so deep.
All I can do is sit and weep.
But tomorrow will come, and peace I might find,
Another burst of strength for my mind,
A new day of sunshine maybe to seek.

ANOTHER BRIDGE

I cannot hide from the past and my sin,
Even though I keep trying to begin again.
No matter what, I will never win.

I thought that finally I could find some peace,
From that monster I'd get some release.

But the monster is back,
And it's me he wants to attack.

I cannot win and I cannot hide.
His hold is strong on my soul where he does reside.

I've made this monster from the web I've created,
What is left of my life that's been wasted.

I try and try to make something new,
But it's not worth the fight; my days are few.

I'm so tired of this fight that I'm losing.
I can't take anymore of the accusing and abusing.

If all I want to do is love,
Why does it feel like only pain falls from above?

I have nothing to look forward to in tomorrow.
I am swallowed by my sorrow.

The monster is clawing and dragging me under.
The feeling is familiar though it makes me shudder.

I never wanted to go back to that place,
But I look in the mirror and I see that face.

The face is of a woman broken.
Only cries from her lips are spoken.

Grieving for another loss,
Another bridge to have to cross.

CHAPTER 5
Destination: Peace

On Super Bowl Sunday 2009, I met Jimmy. He was visiting California with his friend Larry who owns a condo just a few miles away from me. We met at a sports bar where the game was playing. I was only going to be there briefly, but once I met Jimmy, time seemed to slip away quickly. Before we knew it, the game was over. I stayed and had dinner with him and Larry. Jimmy and I became inseparable from that point on.

I fell truly and deeply in love with Jimmy, like I never thought I would ever feel again. We had everything in common and found a strong connection to one another. Jimmy is from New York where he lives on Long Island. He is retired from the NYPD. He is an amazingly strong, intelligent, witty, talented person. It didn't take long to realize that it was a gift that we had found each other. It was a slight inconvenience that we lived on opposite sides of the country, but we seemed to manage pretty well. Since he is retired and I am on a school schedule, we were able to travel back and forth between California and New York regularly enough to maintain a healthy relationship, until recently, when Jimmy relocated here to the desert where we now live together.

What follows, are all poems written to or about Jimmy. There are three that were written after an argument that we had; they are just as important to include because of the emotion that they express. Beside the fact that it would be deceiving to say that in a new relationship there were no bumps in the road here and there. Of course there were; it is all part of learning about each other and learning to communicate.

SO THAT I MAY LIVE

The words on my lips, you know what they are.
My heart tells the truth, though there are scars.
Memories of my pain are never too far.

Can you take my pain away?
I see you now, but will you stay?

This dose I take is bittersweet,
But with not a thought I will take it and eat.
The reward is there for me to greet.

You I have seen in my dreams.
You calmed me and silenced all my screams.

The feelings I thought I would never have again,
Maybe at last I can try to begin.

To give all the love in my heart to you;
If I gave it to you, what would you do?
Would you be so careful like it was something brand new?

The look in your eyes tells me you know.
Now all I need is for you to show.

Show me the love that is in your heart;
The love that I know I never want to part.

I know it is there for you to give.
Breathe it into me so that I may live.

Of this life of mine I will give you my all;
Though on my knees through life I sometimes did crawl.
I promise you, this time I will stand tall.

You have seen in my eyes the way I look at you.
Eyes cannot lie; to you they will always be true.

Separate from you, I am not whole.
But destiny has its course; there is a goal.

Fill me up with the love you can give.
I am here, I am waiting; in you I want to live.

LEAVE MY HEART

How do you go from love to hate?
Do you remember what we said about fate?

The softness when you look at me is gone now.
The depth in your eyes would take my breath away
somehow.
Now they scare me; I have to look down.

The longing for your touch again aches within me.
Can you see me tremble? Touch me, feel me…

Your wall is up; there is no way in.
Just let go! This fight we can win!
But you are lost … lost to my sin.

You were right; they will all walk away
Even you … just look at us today.
You don't even have anything to say.
I know you … nothing will stand in your way.

I put my heart on the line, and I lost.
And for it I paid a pretty high cost.

This is tearing me up; what can I do?
I've given my all to you.

So, now where do we go from here?
I'm scared; I can feel you turn when I come near.
What is in you? Is it hate or fear?
What happened to the love you once whispered in my ear?

I'm going to shut my eyes now and close my mind;
Turn from the dreaded feeling I feel inside.
Try to close the hole that has left me open wide.
Just go now; leave my heart at the bedside.

I'LL BE LOVING YOU

When the wind is whipping through the trees,
And the sound of your voice is lost in the breeze…
I'll be loving you.

When the sky is dark and turning gray,
And you don't know why I would want to stay…
I'll be loving you.

When my tears fall and I am sad,
Because I know I have made you mad…
I'll be loving you.

When you reach for me in the dark of night,
And I am not there in the morning light...
I'll be loving you.

When the moon stands high in the sky,
And you know we have to say good-bye...
I'll be loving you.

When angry words have been said,
And you feel so messed up in your head...
I'll be loving you.

When you look at me with fear and doubt,
And wonder what it's all about...
I'll be loving you.

When you don't know how far to go,
And what emotions you should show...
I'll be loving you.

When I'm not there and you long for me,
And it's in my arms that you want to be...
I'll be loving you.

When you wonder if I still care,
And want to know if I'll be there...
I'll be loving you.

When the day comes that the end is near,
I promise you, have nothing to fear, because...
I'll still be loving you.

TIME STOOD STILL TODAY

Time stood still today.
My heart was heavy,
So much to weigh.

I was reaching and reaching.
Sadness was taking me under.
Do you know what I'm seeking?

I see you and long for your touch.
It's an ache in me.
The need is so much.

Your eyes gaze at me.
The look is pleading.
They mimic my own; don't you agree?

I'm on my knees, face to the floor.
What is this pain?
I don't want to feel it anymore.

The pain is in you, too.
That does not escape me.
Look at us suffer, me and you.

But the love we have is very true.
It is strong and intense.
It doesn't matter that it is new.

Give me your all.
Don't hold back.
I promise you won't fall.

Baby, I can't walk away.
Don't you see?
All I want is to stay.

I'm putting my trust in you.
My heart's on the line.
It's in your hands; what will you do?

Fate has put us in this place.
Look in my eyes.
See the love on my face?

No other will ever compare.
My course is set.
It's you whose life I want to share.

Take the love I want to give.
I give it all.
Just love me back and live.

Live a life of peace with me.
Our souls are intertwined.
You know that we are meant to be.

WALK WITH ME

You walked with me.
You talked with me.
You held my hand.
Now it seems we are in sinking sand.

I'm slipping.
I'm sliding.

You're turning away.
The look in your eye tells me you might not stay.
I blink back the tears as the day turns to gray.

I'm fighting to hold to what used to be.
I'm reaching for you; do you still want me?
For us it's not too late; don't you see?

Touch my face; it is wet with my tears.
Hold me close and calm my fears.
Whisper to me that we have so many years.

Think about what I used to mean to you,
Because back then there was nothing that I wouldn't do.
And together as one we both grew.

This life only takes; it has nothing to give.
In each other is where we promised to live.

How can a love that once was just be gone?
What have we done that was so wrong?

Open your heart and find me there.
Reach for me in the dark where we might meet
somewhere.
There must be a part of you that will still care.

My heart is still yours; I've not taken it back.
I'll leave it with you; you don't have to ask.

So much ahead of our lives to share.
Can we both say that we want to be there?

What will it take to have it all again?
Give me your hand; let's walk, let's talk, and let's begin.

IF YOU WERE ALL I HAD

If I ask you to believe, will you question me?
Believe that my soul is no longer free?

What if I ask you to trust the things I say?
To trust that my love is here to stay?

Do you believe that two souls can really meet?
That passion can grow in the midst of its heat?

If you opened my heart, do you know what you'll find?
Open your eyes to me; don't be blind.

Could your heart hold all the love I have for you?
It would overflow with the bounty; what would you do?

Will you hold me close and not let go?
Tell me all the things I need to know?

When I whisper in your ear, will you kiss my face?
Will you promise no one will take my place?

Do you know how I feel when you say you love me?
Like everything, now is just as it should be.

If I say I long for you when you are away,
Would you run or would you stay?

In the dark of the night when I reach for you,
It comforts me to feel you reach for me, too.

Can you feel my eyes on you and the love they give?
Draw close to me; our life together I want to live.

How do you add up the days of forever?
Because forever means I could leave you never.

Are you asking and wondering why?
Why it is that I sometimes cry?

The thought of life without you makes me sad.
I could live without anything but you, if you were all I
had.

A SILENT MOAN

You dig, and you tear at my skin.
What is in you that makes you have to win?
You constantly throw in my face my sin.

My eyes grow weary from the tears they shed.
I want to go run and hide in my bed.
Do you even remember the things that you said?

The anger in you is a ball of consuming fire.
The words from your mouth keep calling me a liar.

My head, it screams from the agony inside.
Away from your eyes, I feel the need to hide.
Under their stares no longer can I abide.

My hands tremble as I write these words.
Their sounds echo and can barely be heard.

My fucking heart has exploded in my chest.
The burning won't stop; it gives no rest.
Stop fucking with me! Is this a test?

Just go away, and let me be.
You're destroying me; can't you see?
What is it that you want from me?

To love you is all I wanted to do.
I actually thought you loved me, too.
But you really don't, do you?

You fucked me up and got in my face.
I guess I just got put in my place.
I'll turn and go, a whore in disgrace.

That's how you'll leave me, a fucked-up mess.
But you don't care; I've always been less.

No other will get my heart; I won't do this again.
I can't take this; it's gonna do me in.
When will I be free of this sin?!

My head feels heavy with the pain.
If I bleed, it would only be in vain.
But maybe there would be peace to gain.

You'll be gone soon; I'll be all alone.
It's coming from the depths of me, a silent moan.

Understandably, a lot of our arguments had to do with my past behavior resulting from my bipolar, especially in the beginning when we were still getting to know each other. I was torn between what to share with him and what not too because I did not want to be deceitful or give him any surprises later. Jimmy found some of the things I told him a bit overwhelming and shocking, of course, but he saw things through. There certainly were times when he would leave and go back to New York after a visit, and I was sure that was the last time I would ever see him, but he always came back. As our relationship progressed, he became more and more educated about bipolar disorder. He also grew to know me better as a person and my commitment to my wellness, and the fact that I am *not* my illness, I merely suffer from *symptoms* of my illness. Of course, even those symptoms are rare now that I have them highly managed.

As a cop, Jimmy worked the downtown streets of New York City; therefore, soft words aren't one of Jimmy's strong points. On my birthday, he made sure I understood before I got my birthday card that he did not write "mushy" stuff in them. He was not a "word" man. But after an argument one night, when I had written the poem "A Silent Moan," he decided that I was not the only one who could express themselves in poetry. Jimmy had found that the artistic, extroverted part of him could produce words of his own to express his feelings. This first poem is what he came up with. I was quite impressed and, of course, very moved, especially knowing how he struggled with my history *and* his love for me as a double-edged sword.

STAY OR GO

You know I love you
But what should I do?
Should I stay or go,
I haven't a clue.

I'm holding onto things in your past,
When I know I have to let them go
And just let them pass.

I think of these things and they cause me pain,
And they make my tears fall like rain.
But somehow I know I have to get off this train.

Because if I don't I will surely crash,
And I know I will lose you,
Like you were never here and gone in a flash.
Which is why I have to make you stop feeling like trash.

But I swear I get this way because I care so much,
And you know how much I long for your touch.

So what would you say
If I told you I want to stay?
Would it make everything better,
And make all the mean things I say go away?

Maybe you could teach me how to forget,
So I could stay and love you without regret.

I also have a past and I know I have sinned,
Which is why I will try hard to get this done.
Because if I have you, I know I have won,
And to think we have only just begun.

James Tonderella

BEAUTY

You are a thing of beauty.
It is all that I see
When I look in your eyes,
You capture my soul and set me free.

The love I have for you
I can't even explain.
So I won't even try,
Because it will always remain.

Sometimes I get angry and try to resist,
But then I stop and realize
That true love can exist.

Your skin is so smooth
And soft to the touch.
It feels so good,
And makes me want you so much.

I guess all I'm trying to say
Is I can't believe you love me this way.
So promise me you will always stay.

Love makes your beauty run so deep,
And I hope you will always be mine to keep.

So stick around,
And let's give it a try.
Because you know and can't deny
That our love will always survive.

James Tonderella

This next poem Jimmy wrote after we had just had a little squabble. We were sitting in a diner late one night in New York. Jimmy was feeling the need to write, and as every writer knows, when you feel the urge, you grab a pen and paper and get it down or it will be lost forever. The only thing he had handy was a paper bag that our leftovers were going in. We sat at that booth for an hour. Jimmy wrote and I sat there in silence, patiently waiting. Not a word was spoken, but it was well worth the wait.

FORGIVENESS

If you leave me now,
I will never be the same.
And what makes it so sad is
I only have myself to blame.

I have so many mixed emotions.
They rise and fall inside of me
Just like the ocean.

How can you say I don't even like you?
When I know if you leave,
I will be nothing but blue.

I know that I'm driving you crazy,
Like a runaway car you can't stop
Because your mind is so hazy.

So if you decide to leave,
It won't be easy.
I would be left to grieve
And feeling so uneasy.

Please change your mind
And tell me you will stay.
My heart hurts so much,
And I can't bear to see you go away.

We've been through all of this before,
And I know you can't take much more.
But sometimes I can't control what I'm feeling.

As if I'm trying to even or settle the score,
I don't want to lose you or ever feel blue.
And I know in my heart
You will always be true.

Once again you taught me a lesson.
I need to stay calm
And lose all my aggression.

Sometimes I feel like
I'm out of control,
And losing you
Would be a heavy toll.

Please believe me when I say
That I never wanted it to be this way.

You're a thing of beauty
That my heart can't resist.
Please don't tell me we've had our last kiss.

I guess what I'm hoping
Is that you can find it in your heart,
A way to forgive me
So we can make a new start.

If you can't I will understand,
And this will be our last stand.

You're such a sweet girl
And never a fake,
But after all,
How much can you take?

But if you feel we must part,
There will always be a hole in my heart.

And I will be in such a lonely place,
Because you I could never replace.

James Tonderella

This is the most recent poem that Jimmy has written me, and although it was obviously after an argument as well (that seems to be the only time I can bring out this creativity in Jimmy), it is actually my favorite one. If you compare it to the first poem that he wrote, you can surely see how his poetry has matured. This is a beautiful poem; I read it often, and each time I enjoy the words like I'm reading them for the first time.

I ASK MYSELF

You taught me so much today,
And I ask myself
How I could ever repay.
And the answer is, I want you to stay.

Let me make it up to you
And show you I will always be true.

I know it's a big chance to take,
But I promise, my love, I will never fake.

The things I've done were so wrong,
But my love for you is very strong.

How could I cause you so much pain,
And make you want to get on that plane?

I've learned I have issues,
As you know we all do.

So let's not let this end,
And I swear I will never pretend.
You're such a good person,
And I feel so bad,
Especially when you give me love I've never had.

So I guess all we can do is give us a try
And hope our love will never die.

James Tonderella

This poem from Jimmy was from a particularly bad fight that we had. It was intensely emotional, and I nearly relapsed after over a year of no cutting. I was so completely overwhelmed with emotion, and I had moved from logical thinking, where I could use my coping skills, to complete dissociation; I went for a kitchen knife. When Jimmy saw what I was about to do, he became very upset. I can still see the helplessness in his eyes—there was absolutely nothing he could do, and he knew it. Fortunately, something about that look jolted me out of my state, and I put the knife back. I swore I would never put him in that position again. I don't remember a time that I ever let anyone actually *see* me cut. It is usually a very private thing for me, and I have never used it to manipulate someone; that is not what it is about. There is usually a sort of tunnel vision, and the rest of the world is very far away. The fact that I hurt Jimmy enough to move him to write these words puts pain in my heart. Yet, it touches me that he could reach into is soul to pull out enough emotion to put his feelings into such stirring words.

TO NOT LOOK BACK

All I feel now is pain,
And my soul is darkened
And filled with disdain,
Like nothing is left to be gained.

But my heart feels different.
It tells me to stay
And to hold you tight
And never let you slip away.

I never mean you any harm,
But when you put that knife to your arm
It was all so very clear.
It was the first time I tasted true fear.

To see that cold steel against your skin,
It made my body tremble and shiver within.

How could I push you to that place?
I felt so helpless and disgraced.

Now my pain has turned to shame,
And I only have myself to blame,
Like a lost soul who has gone insane.

Why do we hurt the one's we love?
Is it to realize
That no one is above,
Or bigger than the sum of our love?

I will try so hard to not look back
And never again put you under attack.
So let's put today in the past
And hope our love will always last.

James Tonderella

Jimmy has been a very positive, healthy influence in my life. He has taught me something that I never got from any other relationship: independence. I have learned from my time with Jimmy to be stronger and more emotionally dependant on myself, and that I don't have to find my identity in the man that I am with. My identity lies within my own self, and I have found more peace and contentment since I have learned this very important lesson. Whereas my relationships with Lee and Ray were destructive to my mental health, my relationship with Jimmy has in a sense empowered me.

The following are poems written to and inspired by Jimmy. He seems to have the ability to evoke endless poems from me. Note the difference in depth of substance and passion, compared to other romantic poems I have written. Jimmy has found parts of me from the deepest corners of my soul. There have been times that while driving, I have needed to pull over and grab a pen and whatever I could find to write on, because words begin to fill my mind. The first poem here is one of my favorites. I wrote this poem after watching a home movie of Jimmy when he was a little boy, and while gazing into his eyes in childhood photos. His innocent little eyes struck me so deeply; I was moved to write about them.

YOUR CHILD'S EYES

I saw your child's eyes today.
My heart turned soft at what they did say.

Gone were the seasoned years of a man,
Now merely a boy who thinks he can.

Can save the world from the dragon's wrath
And sink mighty ships when he takes his bath.

The sweet innocence of a child's way
Is there in your eyes as a bright, new day.

No ugliness of the world have they seen,
Nor anything wicked, vile or mean.

No sadness or loss has taken the place
Of the wisp of hope and faith in that face.

Your eyes are trusting and true,
But this part I still even now … see in you.

Brown and soft, they are looking expectantly.
What new wonders now today will they see?

Someday soon they will see life's pain,
How others can treat with such disdain;
And how in all of this, there is nothing to gain.

Clear with an anxious awaiting smile,
Even if it's only for awhile.

I saw your child's eyes today.
It was a beautiful sight … no mere words can say.

THE MOONLIGHT

It started that night,
The night the moonlight was
Shining on your face.
That was the night I became
Forever lost in your eyes,
Never to return.

Lost in your eyes;
Lost is where I want to stay.

Look into my soul;
Don't ever look away.

Late at night when I watch you sleep,
It's these memories that I want to keep.
And the vision of your eyes
Linger in my mind,
Promises of when you awake.

Soon the morning will come and take you away,
But the scent of you will remain.
And my love for you I can't contain,
So think of me as you go.
For I'll still be here
When the moonlight ends the day.

ETERNAL FIRE

It took half a lifetime to find you,
And what I see in your eyes I know is true.
Gone are the frivolities of my youth,
What matters now is only truth.

Take my hand and come with me;
Let's journey together and be free.
Lost in each other, separate from the rest,
Giving to each other only the best.

The sunlight warms as it touches my skin;
Its telling me now is the time to begin.
Our feet are resting on solid ground;
Look at this love that we have found.

Hold me close; don't let go.

I'll give you all; just let me show,
Show you the love that is in my heart.
For you and I will never again part.

Forever entwined our souls have become;
Our hearts beat together like pounding drums.
Every breath I take is you.
Breathe me in; can you feel it, too?

Maybe now I can find some peace.
My fears and my pain can finally ease.
For your love has given me hope to go on.
The demons of my past can finally be gone.

You've wrapped me in your strength and held tight,
Given me a reason to go on and fight.
Our love is bigger than heaven and earth;
There is no way to tell its worth.

So love me strong and love me true.
Never let our days be few.
I have waited so long to find this day;
Don't ever leave, always stay.

Go on with me till our lives end.
No more wounds to have to mend.
To be with you is my heart's desire;
For the love we have is an eternal fire.

YOUR LOVE SETS ME FREE

I know you're ready to leave my side;

So many things you cannot abide.
I can see you want off this maddening ride.

I know that I am no prize,
And you, you are so wise.
Maybe someday you will realize.

But sometimes love it is a curse.
We want to run; go in reverse.

But sometimes in our lives we've shown
That in so many ways we have grown,
And to ourselves we must own.

And I have found to own is to be free;
Free to give to you a part of me.

This is my choice; I will not turn back,
Even under strife and attack,
When sometimes mercy is what we lack.

When pain seems too much to endure,
And questions make it hard to be sure,
But true love we know is always pure.

One day we will look back and see our path,
With all the tears and all the wrath.

Knowing they were only stones along the way,
Angry words when we didn't know what to say,
But always knowing that we would stay.

I'll wait an eternity for that day to come.
Though patience, I don't know where it will come from.

You are worth every sacrifice to me,
For it's your love that sets me free.

WAIT FOR THE MOMENT

Running blindly in the night; something is chasing me.
It's back again; it's haunting me.
I've lost them all, but will I ever be free?

Do you wonder how much I can take?
I'm falling hard; when I land, I will break.

But you're there; I can see you stretching out your hand.
Will you catch me now, before I land?

I look to the sky; the stars spell your name.
The stars fall upon me as if washing away blame.

Why are you here? I thought you would go,
Gone like the wind on the desert as it blows.
But you're here; what are you trying to show?

To show me the peace you know can be mine?
To tell me you alone my life can define?

In sleep I reach for you and your not there.
All I feel is cold, thin air.
The loneliness shakes me as I lay and stare.

The rhythm of the day moves me to its beat.
But when you're not here, I am not complete.

My burden is heavy like the summer's heat.

I wait for the moment I can touch your face,
Because with all I've lost, you I can't replace.

When you wrap me up and hold me tight,
It makes me feel like I can continue this fight.
Because in your arms all else is right.

Through my battles I will hold up my head
And remember all the things that you said,
And shown me my demons are no longer to dread.

MY WORLD IS RIGHT

Standing in the darkness, I search for the light.
Then I see your face and everything becomes bright,
Because with you, my world is right.

The safety I find is in your arms.
There is where I know I am free from harm.

When you are gone, my longing becomes grief.
It matters not if the time is only brief.
And I fear for the moment that you will leave.

You have touched my soul in places unknown,
And I have seen how our love has shown.
Shown that in every special way, it has grown.

Grown to be something strong and true,
And I know I will never let go of you,
Because we have become one from two.

I sit and think of all the ways you love me
And all the things that I want to be;
To be the one from which you will never want to be free.

All the years that we have past,
They have moved on so very fast.
But what is up ahead, I want each day to last.

To share with you all that is in my heart,
And to open you up and take you apart.

So I can chase away all your fears
And wash away all your tears.

Because joy is what I want you to feel,
And your love to be giving and real,
And our passion to be strong as steel.

All of me is what I give to you.
I will never take it back, no matter what you do.
Life moves fast; our days are so few.

So hold tight and don't let go.
In the trees I can hear the wind blow.
Your mine and I am yours, for this we both know.

COMES THE LIGHT

Some days I've seen how far I've come;
Other days it feels my heart is numb.
Add them together, what is the sum?

Tears on my face are turning to blood.

My feet are sinking in deep, dark mud.

The shadow that follows me crosses your path.
The look on your face is turning to wrath,
Like a hurricane leaves the aftermath.

Why is it that I'm to blame?
And why in my soul do I have to feel shame?

But the shame I feel is not from you,
And the blame I have, it comes from me, too.
And I'm not quite sure what I should do.

To finally be free of the monster's grip,
And from the cup of peace to be able to sip.

I look inside for where I need to be strong
And to know that my journey is still long.
But to give and to love, I can't go wrong.

Just when I thought that love was lost,
You came along and you paid the cost.

The cost it took to set my soul free,
To make it what you wanted it to be.
But I look inside, and I see more than me.

I see children grown and love I've found.
And to hear the words "I love you" is such a sweet sound.

Take my hand and say you won't let go.
Tell me that our lives will grow,
And together in life new seeds we'll sew.

For out of the darkness comes the light,
And everything now, feels just right.

Yes, Jimmy has been a breath of fresh air to my life, and together we have created a safe and happy relationship that I have not had in a very long time. He is the joy and love of my life; his wisdom and strength lift and empower me like no other man has done before. We have been together for just over two years, and each day brings us closer and makes our connection stronger. We are looking forward to a wonderful future together.

Although it had been six years since my initial diagnosis, I had come to a very difficult point in my life with my children. I came home from a trip to New York one day during the summer of 2009 to a very upsetting speech from my youngest son Daniel. He was addicted to heroin. He was "dope sick" and desperate to get off the drugs. I was immediately thrown into a whirlwind of emergency rooms, detoxing and terrible withdrawals. There were also other behavioral problems, such as stealing, lying, mood swings, not going to school, and getting in trouble with the law. This was not my son; he was a mess. I never thought this would be something I would face with any of my children, yet here I was. I was devastated, hurt, and, of course, guilt-ridden believing that somehow I was the cause because I had not been the mother I should have been for those critical years. Something got missed, and now we were reaping the repercussions from it. I felt all the pain of the withdrawals that he did.

I was also juggling school where I had been maintaining

a near 4.0, with two semesters to go to get my associates degree in psychology. But I had terrible difficulties with math, in which I was barely hanging on with a C at this particular time. In Idaho, my daughter was going through some very difficult problems with her boyfriend ("little man's" daddy) and her dad, so she needed my attention as well.

I began to do research on heroin and found that this was not going to be an easy fight. Heroin topped the list as one of the most difficult drugs to beat. Following are three poems I wrote concerning my children and the immense pressure I was under.

WHEN A MOTHER LOVES

Drained from tasks they set before me,
Do I see up ahead the chance to be free?
Free from the burden they put on me.

A mother's love has neither beginning nor an end.
My will to protect you cannot bend.
But my heart is in pieces; is there no way to mend?

They take away tiny pieces of my heart.
Now I feel all broken apart.
I thought I could do it; I thought I was smart.

Their desire is not to cause me pain.
But do they know my struggle to stay sane?
Sometimes I think it's about their own gain.

I would do all to make their burden light.
Against all evil I would fight;

Calm their fears in the dark of night.

On the day they were born, my course was set.
I played the cards; I made that bet.
I won't give up; I'll pay the debt.

Each beat of their heart echoes my own.
I've seen the world change them as they've grown,
And watched every seed that they have sown.

Many tears I've shed from bitter words from each;
When I felt they were lost and out of my reach;
When battle lines were drawn, only to be breeched.

But a mother's love can never be wrong;
Even when days of sorrow seem so long,
And when all of our songs have been sung.

To each of them my all I will give.
I will stand by them in this life as they live.

For myself, I will never even count the cost.
For when a mother loves, no child is ever lost.

YOU LET GO OF MY HAND

My lips say your name, but there is no sound.
I am searching for you, but you can't be found.
Is that my heart lying on the ground?

Pieces are missing, no way to replace.
You have taken, broken, and thrown them in my face.

Now I'm alone and lost in this place.

Where is the softness and joy in your soul?
You are lost in yourself, a deep dark hole.
I want to save you, but I have lost control.

The web you have spun around you is deep.
If you listen you can hear my soul weep.
Peace eludes me; I no longer sleep.

Voices in my head won't stop their lament.
I can't fight, my strength is gone; I am spent.
I shot the arrow, but it must have bent.

Do you even know the depth of a mother's loss,
To know that her child's line had been crossed?

And to know that he may never return,
And, oh, how her heart does burn.

When all I want is to be near you;
I thought that is what you wanted, too.
But your path has taken you from my view.

The journey you're on is lonely and dark,
Like a burnt down forest whose trees are stark,
Not lush and green as a beautiful park.

I never thought you'd let go of my hand.
Now it seems you are in sinking sand,
And I'm far away in an unknown land.

Someday you'll see the life you've chosen,
And maybe your heart will become unfrozen.

When that day comes, I will be here,
And I'll open my arms and draw you near.
Because your mother I am, whispering I love you, in your
ear.

JUST DISAPPEAR

What would it take to just disappear?
Every breath that I take fights back the tears.
A moment ago, I thought I felt fear.

Hands all around me, dragging me down;
Voices so loud that I can't hear a sound.
Stumbling and falling, my knees on the ground.

Looking for a place to hide,
Trying to find peace on the other side.
Where I am now, I can no longer abide.

They are searching for me, calling my name.
But here I will hide; in my shadow I will remain.
Sad but true, it's all the same.

They are tearing me apart with claws of greed.
It's all about their own need.
It's on me that they wish to feed.

Escape is my only way out.

But my voice is silent, I cannot shout.
Someone please tell me, what is this all about?

Cover my face; don't show that I feel hopeless.
They will only see it as my weakness.

My strength has left me; I can no longer stand.
Where in my life is my protecting hand?
I feel lost and alone in another land.

Escape from the wrath of the monster that haunts me.
The monster inside that won't let me be free.
It controls with guilt and shame of what used to be.
The hands and the monster, they all want a piece of me.

But I have nothing left; they've taken all.
I'm on the edge, ready to fall.
Strength is gone; I can only crawl.

I'm closing down; don't look my way.
What did you say? You're drifting farther away.
What does it take to get peace to stay?

My fight with math progressed, as did Daniel's problems with drugs. Much to my great distress, I had to drop my math class for the second time. I was under an unbearable amount of stress. I had kicked Daniel out of the house after a terrible fight when I found that he had stolen, yet again, more money from me. I could see that his drug use was getting way out of control, and not only was he getting into trouble himself, but he was bringing it around home too. He had made some terrible enemies within his addiction. We had death threats as well as threats of our home being burned down. Even so far as to blowing up my car; I was terrified. Once Daniel was gone, I didn't feel any better, especially when Jimmy was away in New York. I began sleeping on the couch and not in my room, because I thought I could hear what was going on in the house better from the living room. I slept with a knife, a flashlight, and my pepper spray stuffed under the couch cushions. Every time the dogs barked, I shot up off the couch like an alarm went off; running from one window to the next thinking someone was outside my home. Every light outside every door was on; it looked like daytime outside my house.

I had no idea where Daniel was living or what he was doing. He dropped by now and then to do laundry or just to visit with me, but I didn't ask questions because I really didn't want to know the answers. He looked terrible. He was skinny, his face was all picked over, and his eyes were large and sunk into his head like a ghost. I knew he was in bad shape. I even went through his backpack one day and found exactly what I thought I would: drug paraphernalia. It was heroin.

I left to go to New York for Thanksgiving. I no sooner landed on the runway and turned on my phone when it rang; it was the alarm company to the new alarm we had just installed in my house before I had left. My alarm was going off. It had been breached, but my house had not been broken into, yet the motion detector was set off inside the house. I could only think that it must have been Daniel. He was an expert at getting into the house, and he had no idea that there was a motion detector on the inside. Yet, I still was hesitant to blame him. There will always be so many unanswered questions.

No sooner had I returned from my trip eight days later, the day after Thanksgiving, that I received a phone call from Daniel. He was in some trouble, but he wouldn't say what. The next day I found out that he had been arrested. He was in jail for carrying an open pocket knife, a felony in California. I knew what was coming. It only took a few hours; he began calling me, begging me to get him out. He was starting to come down, and he needed drugs. The family got together on the phone to discuss what we were going to do with him. We all decided that we were not going to bail him out. He was going to stay there until his arraignment five days later. This was his wake-up call. Oh my, I did not know what I was in for. I had seen Daniel come down once before, and it was not pretty. I knew it would be terrible for him to go through it in jail. My mother's instinct to protect and care for her child was kicking in, yet I had to check myself; tough love was in order. He had access to a phone, and he used it. He called me over and over and over; crying and begging me to get him out. It was one of the worst things I had ever had to go through with one of my children. He was hurting, and I couldn't help him. I had to stop answering the phone, but I listened to it ring, knowing that it was him on the other end wanting me.

By about the third day, he was feeling better. He had gone to the hospital because of the withdrawals he was going through, so that helped him a bit. Our biggest problem at that point was what to do when he got out. I couldn't take him back home, and we didn't want to send him back out to the streets. We had to find him a program to go into. Money was an issue, and a state program was going to be approximately a four-month waiting list, and not very highly recommended at that. He was too young and it would be a harsh environment for him. My mom, bless her again, found him a place in Northern California. It was a private residence that he would be in for four to six months, and it was going to cost thirty thousand dollars. Once again my family pulled together and pitched in to save one of their own. This time it wasn't me; it was my son.

There is one person in this family that everyone has the utmost respect for and no one will cross, not even Daniel. That person is my dad. So, that was who broke the news to him when he got out of jail. My dad picked him up at midnight, took him home to sleep a few hours at his house, and at 7:00 AM the next morning, I was driving Daniel to the airport to go to his new home for the next four months. He was grateful. That was all we wanted to hear.

Here are two poems I wrote for Daniel.

BEGIN AGAIN

Where did yesterday's smile go,
And all the days I watched you grow?
I guess the answers I will never know.

Do you see the path that your life is on?
Where will you be in the coming dawn?
Your face looks old, weathered, and drawn.

Choices made, now paying the price.
You thought you'd win when you rolled that dice.
Now your eyes have gone dark, cold as ice.

I tried to save you; you know I did.
But you walked away; you turned and hid.
The son I knew, he is gone, a life wasted.

But you see your course; you determine your fate.
You can be free; it's not too late.

Love you I do; but I can only wait.

Wading through waste of a shattered life,
Now all you feel is pain and strife.
In your heart you feel the sting of that knife.

The monster's claws are strong and deep.
This I see, and it makes me weep.
Your eyes are open; you no longer sleep.

From the monster, you try to run and hide.
But by your choice, he remains by your side.
His mouth is waiting to draw you inside.

But you have a choice, you can still be free.
From the monster you can flee.
I know you are not where you want to be.

Reach for me and take my hand,
Because by me I know you can stand.
My strength I'll give you; on your feet you will land.

Yet, in yourself you must find
What it will take to stop and rewind;
To no longer be walking as if blind.

To seek the truth of whom you are,
And to know that your journey is still yet far,
And it's okay if there is a scar.

Because in this life you can win.
It's not really about your sin.
Stop now … look around;

It's time to begin again.

WHEN THE WIND BLOWS

Last night, I dreamt of you in my sleep.
I thought I lost you, and it made me weep.

It's hard to understand that I can't save you.
It's something that only you can do.

But you can know how much I care;
And that it's true that I will always be there.

From my own body you were born,
And to the Creator you were sworn.

And it is Him that we must trust.
And though we fear, we know He is just.

So focus on your journey ahead.
Be strong, like a man; don't hide in your bed.

Take every challenge as a battle to beat.
For to win the war would be a great feat.

I know in my heart that this you can do,
Because to your heart you must be true.

Integrity and dignity are what you now lack,
But you will see your journeys end when you get them
back.

As David did with Goliath, be courageous and stand firm.
Don't give in to your fear, nor just hide and squirm.

You're an amazing person, talented and smart.
Are you ready now to make this new start?

It's time to put the boy away.
Let the man out; now never to betray.

Take the hard road; you will learn the most.
Turn and confront; don't just hide from your ghosts.

Each new trial will make you strong.
I promise you; these words will not be wrong.

A mother's love is beyond measure,
A love that is worth more than any treasure.

Take my words and hold them close.
And hear my voice say, "I love you," when the wind blows.

As of this writing, Daniel completed four months of his program with success and has remained drug free for over a year. He is living with his dad in Idaho and will not be returning to the desert where I am, because we do not want him near any of his old friends who are still dealing with their own addictions. We feel very lucky to have caught Daniel's drug problem so soon and to have had such a strong support network of family and friends. Daniel himself has a great attitude, is very motivated, and is doing great. I have all the hope in the world that he will remain successful. He is young and has a whole life ahead of him. He is working;

sometimes more than one job at a time, and is very driven to succeed in life.

Daniel does show very strong symptoms of bipolar disorder, though, which is not a surprise, and this is something that we need to focus on now. I am confident that he is ready to realize that this is another obstacle in his life to deal with and that the sooner he does, the easier his future will be. Sarah has done very well beginning to manage her bipolar, and I think Daniel will, too. Jacob is glad that he has escaped that gene in the family gene pool! I am glad that Sarah and Daniel both have the opportunity to begin management of their illness at such a young age, unlike me who had to wait until thirty-six!

I endure one sadness that plagues my heart every moment of every day, my son Jake. I believe that I hurt all my children because of symptoms of my illness, but I think Jake might have been affected more so in a different way. I have three possible guesses: Jake's sensitivity, the relationship he had with me, and the fact that when I left Idaho I took Daniel with me and not him. Although Jake chose not to come, in his mind that would not have mattered; I was splitting him up from his brother, and in a way, I was abandoning him. I may never know whether I am right or not, because Jake won't talk about these things with me. Yet, it breaks my heart when I see Jake. Although he will talk to me, he still keeps himself disconnected. He won't talk to me at all when I am at home in California; no phone calls, texting, nothing. When I see him in pictures, I look into eyes and see only things a mother can see … and it breaks my heart. I believe it is my fault. No, I *know* it is my fault.

I guess lately this has been weighing heavy on my mind; I had a dream about Jake one night. I was given the chance to go back and raise my children all over again, undo every regret I have. (Wouldn't that be nice?) I was lying in bed, Jake must have been about five or so, and he climbed into bed with me. This was one of those extremely vivid dreams where all your senses are so sharp that you can truly experience the dream, or so it seems. Jake told me he was afraid and wanted to sleep with me. I pulled him close and told him there was nothing to fear, and of course he could sleep with me. I held him, stroked his red hair, kissed him on the forehead, and just snuggled with him. I could smell his soft, childlike smell, the smell of the baby shampoo in his hair, and feel the softness of his skin as a rubbed his back. And I began to cry. That was when I awoke; crying. Now, this was not an unusual scene; I was extremely affectionate to my children. I hugged and kissed on them all the time, but patience wasn't one of my strong points. Thus, the message I got from the dream was to just stop and attend to his needs with peace, not the anxiety that I always felt while I was raising my children. There was never a shortage of love and affection, but patience? Now *that* was a hard one for me at times. Although, I have to keep things in perspective by reminding myself that I was a very young mother with an undiagnosed mental illness. Yet, as I see the suffering that my children have had to endure because of my illness, the guilt and remorse can be so overwhelming. I wish I could take them now and hold them close and take away all the pain and fears that I gave them. I hope that in time, Jake will come to see the big picture and be able to find forgiveness in his heart for me. This poem is about Jake.

PEACE WITHIN

In my heart, there is a headstone that bares your name.
And though you're not dead, you're gone just the same.
And here I sit, alone with my shame.

On me you've turned your back,
And its mercy that you lack.

On the day you were born, our souls were bound.
And now our hearts are broken; scattered on the ground.
I'm screaming, but you can't hear a sound.

For I am the one who gave you life.
But you've taken mine, and left me with your anger and
strife.

All because I stumbled and fell,
Lying at the bottom of deep, dark well.

I reach to touch you, but you disappear.
Not wanting me, so deep in your fear.
Shutting me out, not wanting me near.

Ghosts from the past continue to haunt,
Memories that still taunt.

Yet, peace is only found in forgiveness.
And don't you know that it's you that I miss?
So many years wasted in ugliness.

You are my son, my "simple man."
The life we have was not my plan.

Someday maybe you will see the light.
Maybe then you will give up this fight,
Stop the monsters that plague your night.

I will be here waiting for you

And loving you, no matter what you do.

If I could go back, you know I would
Do all the things I know I should.
But the monster had me, covered my face like a hood.

Please come back to me, my son.
There are so many victories to be won,
So many wrongs to be undone.

Open your heart and let me back in.
Look deep, my son; find your peace within.

This next poem is a favorite one of my nephew Dustin, and I think it is appropriate to put near the end. Erik Erikson's (a well-known psychologist) describes the stages of development over the lifespan. At the ages of forty to fifty, we come to a stage that Dr. Erikson calls Generactivity versus Stagnation. In this stage, we find that we stop and take a look at our lives and see where we are at. Are we happy in our careers? Our relationships? Where do we go from here, and are we happy with the direction that our life is moving in? This is the stage where a lot of middle-aged people make career changes and set a new pattern for their futures; taking stock and seeing if they are showing productivity in their lives. Their children are grown, or nearly so, and some (like me) may even have grandchildren at this point. Stagnation is where we don't make any changes that may need to be made, and we just stay stagnant or in a rut. We might continue to be unhappy and never do anything to make it better. I feel as if I have gotten to that point in my life. All my children have left the home, I have started a new career by going back to school to study psychology, I am in a healthy relationship, and I am at a good place concerning my bipolar disorder. My meds are good; I go to my psychiatrist and therapist regularly and practice my coping skills. Although I am going through some difficulties with my children, I maintain my health by remembering to keep it as top priority in my life. I can't help the one's I love in my life if I am not working at optimum condition first.

EMBRACE THE DAY

The days they move without a sound,
Until the day comes when you have found

All that you had you have spent.
And all the love you had, you have sent.

You look around at what you've done.
Where are the prizes that you have won?
They have disappeared like the setting sun.

The ones you loved have gone away.
The ones who said they would always stay.

Another corner your life has turned;
What this time have you earned?

A place in the sun to sit and bask?
Or will you put back on that mask?

People hide behind their smile,
But yours you have put away for awhile.

Will you ever get back that chance?
Place a bet on another romance?

Yet, your heart has been broken so many times,
As you've said over and over in these rhymes.

So, where do you go from here?
Your course is set; the end is near.
Embrace the day; there's no need to fear.

My goal in writing this book and sharing my journey with you was to offer insight into the bipolar mind with the hope that there would be those out there that could relate to my experiences. The first step in dealing with a mental illness is getting past the denial. Seeing your own symptoms in someone else can help to deal with that denial by saying, "Hey, I'm not the only one out there with a messed up head!" Having a mental illness is a heavy burden, but with a strong desire to be well, a good doctor, a good therapist, and a good support system, chances of success are very high. And let me express the importance of a good therapist. I even now continue to see a therapist. It is someone to keep me grounded and on track, always watching for symptoms that I may not notice myself. As of yet, though, I have never found a therapist as perfect for me as Lori, because we connected so well with each other. I will always be so grateful to her.

Since bipolar disorder affects everyone so differently, each and every journey will be very different. To persevere and realize it is not only for yourself, but for those around you who love you and need you, it is a battle that can be won.

I have also addressed, quite frankly, my cutting disorder. If you or a loved one is battling with this, please, please seek professional help that pertains directly to this issue. It could possibly be a life-saving decision. Don't ever underestimate a cutter; they may start with very minor forms of self-harm, but it can become grossly out of control if the emotional issues are not resolved. Statistically, 97 percent of cutters have had sexual abuse in their past. Contrary to popular belief, *most* cutters do NOT cut as a way to get attention. Quite the contrary actually; it is usually a very private form of self punishment, and rarely does a cutter want to discuss their wounds or why and how they got there. Remember also that with self-punishment comes feelings of shame, guilt, and even self-loathing. Dealing with a cutter is a very sensitive matter. Cutting is also not the only form of self punishment. Burning, pulling out hair and picking or scratching off skin are others though less common.

I share two final poems with you, and they are appropriate in closing; a closing to what I have described to you as my journey, both past and present. I have seen many things and have had many experiences; all at some sort of cost, but paid for by lessons learned. I do not know what is around the next corner, but I do know that I am strong enough to endure whatever is to come; if not by my own strength then by the love of those around me and above. Be strong on your own journey and know that each test of endurance will only make you better and stronger if you let it.

THE PATH

As I look back and see how I've grown,
I can see how my life has shown;
Shown how I've won and lost,
Both with a heavy cost.
But now I see all along I've known.

Known that love has always consumed me,
And that love is what it takes to be free;
Free from the past and all the pain.
For in pain there is nothing ever to gain.
To find peace and give love is my true destiny.

So many people I've seen come and go;
Child's faces as I've watched them grow,
With all the hopes of the world to see
And all the things that they want to be.
But the days go by and the memories blow.

So much regret, guilt, and shame;
For all of that, what is the name?
A life lived as time marches by?
The wind on the leaves breathes a heavy sigh.
Sometimes it all just feels like a game.

The future looms as a desolate road.
The journey continues as I carry my load.
But I gather my courage and face the night;
Nothing will stop me from continuing this fight,
Though sometimes it feels like the world will explode.

Peace and fulfillment are in my reach.
And to those I love, my all to each.
It's finally time to make peace with my past.
The monster inside will no longer last,
From mistakes to learn and to others to teach.

To teach what I have found to be true.
And in weakness now know what to do.
To see the path that I have walked,
And unlock the chains that once were locked,
And to see my life with a new clear view.

JOURNEY'S END

Visions before me roll like the sea.
There is peace within for what is to be.

The path I have chosen is already laid.
The past is forgotten, though regrets I've made.

I've loved and lost along the way.
Though to choose again, on this path would I stay?

I cannot answer for my end is unknown.
My conclusion is still yet unshown.

So to love and lose again I will feel,
For this in life I know to be real.

My heart I will give to those of each
I was given in life to show and to teach.

And my soul shall belong to its only mate,

For I know that this shall fulfill my fate.

And the peace that I have struggled for
Will be opened to me from behind that door.

And at journey's end, when I cross that line,
I will realize that victory is mine.

Peace&Love

SUGGESTED READING

Castle, Lana R. *Bipolar Disorder Demystified; Mastering the Tightrope of Manic -Depression.* New York: Marlowe and Company, 2003.

Duke, Patty. *A Brilliant Madness; Living with Manic-Depressive Illness.* New York: Bantam Books, 1992.

Jan Fawcett, M.D., Bernard Golden, Ph.D., & Nancy Rosenfeld. *New Hope for People with Bipolar Disorder.*New York: Three Rivers Press, 2007.

Miklowitz, David J. *The Bipolar Disorder Survival Guide.* New York: The Guilford Press, 2002.

NATIONAL ALLIANCE ON MENTAL ILLNESS

(NAMI)

(800) 950-NAMI or http://www.nami.org

This organization is the strongest advocate for the mentally ill in the country. Its goals are to educate the public on all aspects of mental illness in the family network, to provide awareness and support to those afflicted and their families, and to advocate politically by giving the mentally ill a voice in society.

Mental illness is so very misunderstood and plagued by fierce negative opinion and stereotypes, but NAMI reaches out to reduce discrimination and knock down the barriers that keep those with mental illness from getting the treatment that is so imperative to a positive quality of life.

I sincerely encourage everyone, family, friends, and those battling with their own mental illness, to research NAMI and use its resources to help and offer guidance in maintaining one's own health.

ACKNOWLEDGMENTS

My deepest gratitude for all of those who believed in me and helped to make the publishing of this book possible:

Chuck and Linda Anderson
Trisha, Kelly, Dustin and Zac Archer
James Tonderella
Iva Phillips
Emma and Larry Gotthardt
Juan Carlos Paz
Becky O'Brien
Sandy LeFlore
Mary Payne
Daisy Sanchez
Suzanne and Jim Hollister
Elaine Henderson
Larry Miller
Bryan Wright
Marlene and Tim Archer
Deniece and Tony Young
Lynne Warberg
Ryan Giese
Judy and Paul Magana
Chuck Sellers
Sandy and Norm Pariseau
Tom Carson
Stephanie Colt
Vicki Caldwell
Mona Scaffide

Special acknowledgement to Lori Johnson, the one who found me, picked me up, and pushed me forward.